FRESH FAITH

FRESH FAITH

WHAT HAPPENS WHEN REAL FAITH IGNITES GOD'S PEOPLE

JIM CYMBALA

PASTOR OF THE BROOKLYN TABERNACLE

WITH DEAN MERRILL

ZondervanPublishingHouse

Grand Rapids, Michigan

A Division of HarperCollinsPublishers

Fresh Faith
Copyright © 1999 by Jim Cymbala

Requests for information should be addressed to:

ZondervanPublishingHouse
Grand Rapids, Michigan 49530

Library of Congress Cataloging-in-Publication Data

Cymbala, Jim, 1943-
     Fresh faith: what happens when real faith ignites God's people/ Jim
Cymbala with Dean Merrill.
       p. cm.
Includes bibliographical references.
     ISBN 0-310-23007-1
     1. Fresh.   I. Merrill, Dean.   II. Title.
BV4637.C96 1999
243—dc21   99-35508
                                                                                    CIP

This edition printed on acid-free paper.

Interior design by Sherri L. Hoffman

Printed in the United States of America

00 01 02 03 04 05 06 /❖ DC/ 10 9 8 7 6

Contents

PART 1

~

Something Is Missing

ONE

～

Stolen Property

I LIVE IN A CITY where things get stolen all the time. Along Flatbush Avenue, where our church is, car thefts are an everyday occurrence. So are muggings, purse snatchings, and apartment break-ins.

Once in a Sunday night sermon I made the mistake of asking our congregation to raise their hands if they had personally experienced some kind of rip-off. The place broke into laughter as 98 percent of the hands went up. What a silly question to pose to a crowd of New Yorkers!

My wife, Carol, and I live in the borough of Queens, east of LaGuardia Airport and Shea Stadium, where the Mets play. I came out to my car parked in front of our house one morning a few years ago and noticed it had been vandalized. As soon as I opened the door and got inside, I saw a huge, gaping hole in the center of the steering wheel where the air bag had been.

Crack cocaine addicts love air bags because they are a quick-sale item. Within minutes they can walk into a "chop shop"—an illicit garage that deals in used auto parts—and trade an air bag for up to $200 cash. It is just one of the ways that crack has devastated New York and other major cities in America. Heroin was one thing, snorting cocaine another—but crack has brought massive destruction.

I moaned to myself about the loss. When I called my insurance agent, he took it in stride. "Well, that's the Big Apple for you," he said. "Happens all the time." We filled out the claims paperwork and ordered the part from the dealer. I didn't ask what this would do to my rates next time around; I didn't really want to know.

A few months passed before I finally got around to taking the car in for the replacement. At last the damage was repaired.

And wouldn't you know—within three weeks I got ripped off again! Same parking place in front of my house, same window forced open. I'm almost sure it was the same thief.

This time I didn't even bother to file an insurance claim. I just paid the $800 for replacement out of my pocket rather than risk my rates going through the roof.

I even found a way to joke about it with someone: "You know, maybe I should leave coffee and cake for this guy on the front seat ... with a note that says, 'Hey, let's be friends! If I'd just supply you with other stuff to sell, at least you wouldn't have to break into my car every few months.'"

MORE THAN MERCHANDISE

FORTUNATELY, AIR BAGS CAN be replaced. As much as you hate the loss and inconvenience, you gradually go on with your life. A year later, you won't even remember that it happened.

But in the spiritual realm, a kind of stealing is going on in many lives that is much more serious. Satan is in the business of ripping off things far more important than an air bag. That is his nature. As Jesus said in John 10:10, "The thief comes only to *steal* and kill and destroy."

Satan obviously doesn't want car parts. Nor does he want your house; he doesn't live in a house. He doesn't need your vehicle, for he has other modes of transportation. He has no interest in your clothes; he's a spirit being. He doesn't care about your investments; what would money mean to him?

> **In the spiritual realm, a kind of stealing is going on in many lives. Satan is in the business of ripping us off. ～**

But he is very interested in stealing *spiritual treasures*—things that have value with God and are of eternal significance. Take, for example, our very purpose for living. Satan loves snatching men and women on the streets of my city and your city—people who have potential—and turning them into glassy-eyed wanderers through life, with no goal from day to day. They lie in bed at night staring at the ceiling, saying, "What's the point? Just to make money? Just to have kids? Why?"

People turn to drugs and alcohol because they don't have a clue as to why they're alive. Others turn to career achievement, or pleasure, or materialism . . . something, anything to fill the void. But it doesn't work. God created them to worship and enjoy him forever, but this awareness has been stolen from their consciousness.

Notice the progression in John 10:10. Satan's first move is just petty larceny. Once he manages that, he can move on to actual killing, and from there to mass destruction. "Steal . . . kill . . . destroy." But it all starts with stealing.

WHAT HAPPENED TO "FIRST LOVE"?

EVEN AMONG THOSE WHO are Christians, the devil has a strategy of theft. For example, as a pastor I have seen over and over the tragic loss of our *"first love"* for Jesus. There was a time in our lives when we loved Jesus so much more than we do today. Our appetite for God's Word was voracious. Our love for God's house was enthusiastic. Our eagerness for spreading the gospel was so strong.... Now, how is it? Yes, we still love the Lord. We still come to church. But what happened to all that energy and passion?

That is the problem Jesus addressed with the Ephesian church in Revelation 2:2–5: "I know your deeds, your hard work and your perseverance.... Yet I hold this against you: You have forsaken your first love. Remember the height from which you have fallen! Repent and do the things you did at first. If you do not repent, I will come to you and remove your lampstand from its place."

Where does "first love" go? Our zeal and our intensity don't evaporate. Satan steals the hot embers of devotion and consecration. We get ripped off.

> **The Bible has no retirement plan. God can keep his people on fire for him, keep them sharp and intense.** ~

Someone might say, "Well, you have to understand that back when I met Christ, I was an energetic teenager. A lot has happened since then. You know, we all mellow out with time." Does anyone really believe that? The Bible says God's plan for us is that we be "transformed into his likeness with *ever-increasing* glory, which comes from the Lord, who is the Spirit" (2 Corinthians 3:18). There is no end to the power he wants to exhibit in our lives. The Bible has no retirement plan. God can keep his people on fire for him, can keep them sharp and intense. We need to be honest and admit what has really happened. There is no point in conning ourselves. We've been ripped off by the master thief.

FADED CALLING

OR HOW ABOUT THAT unique *calling* that rests on every Christian's life—the gifting to serve others in the name of the Lord? Ten years ago there was a stirring inside of you; he gave you a dream about what he wanted to do in your life. Maybe he wanted you to teach children. Maybe he wanted you to sing. Maybe he wanted you to be a prayer warrior, standing in the gap for other people in need. Maybe there was even a pull toward the mission field that was birthed by the Holy Spirit himself.

But then ... you got discouraged. Somebody let you down. Something went sour at your church. You tried once or twice, but somebody criticized you. Soon the dream was gone, and the calling wasn't so real. All the inspiration you had felt was missing.

Sometimes I meet pastors in this condition—a hollow shell of their former selves. All the energy is gone; they're just going through the ministerial motions now.

You would tend to imagine this happening mainly through the many discouragements that ministers face and their over-burdened schedules leading to burnout. Actually, those are only two of Satan's strategies for going after the shepherds who work among God's flock. He has many others as well.

Years ago I met a man who really seemed sincere as he labored tirelessly to build up a congregation of believers in a major city. God's blessing upon his preaching was evident. The church began to flourish.

A few years later, I happened to visit one of his services. Something had obviously changed. The pastor had somehow come to believe that *he* was special. The spotlight was now more on him than on Jesus Christ. The messenger had tragically become bigger than the message.

We chatted afterward, and he pointedly asked me what I sensed about the direction of his church. I encouraged him as best I could, but then added, "Remember, my friend— don't take yourself too seriously. This is about God's Spirit working in the lives of people to draw them nearer to Jesus. We're just called to serve them. Preach the Word faithfully, and then disappear into the background so God will get all the praise."

He didn't seem very excited about my last remarks.

His limited fame seemed to go quickly to his head, and soon the simple sincerity and childlike faith that had characterized his earlier efforts for God were replaced by a slick, affected flamboyance, which is very destructive to the cause of Christ. The man's effective preaching and spiritual fruit quickly disappeared.

Where do you think they all went? Something very precious was stolen along the way.

The devil is always trying to rob us of something God blessed us with. When he succeeds, the spiritual gifts seem to fade, and the material things occupy our attention twenty-four hours a day.

Home Burglaries

Consider the subject of marriage. The latest surveys by researcher George Barna show that the divorce rate among churchgoers is just about equal with the population at large. If I were an atheist or an agnostic, I'd say, "Look—how come Jesus can't keep you two together? I thought you said he was so wonderful. . . ."

Why are Christian couples breaking up? Is it because they shouldn't have gotten married in the first place? Or because they came from dysfunctional homes and had bad role models? There is more to it than that. *The thief comes to steal....*

> **The divorce rate among churchgoers is just about equal with the population at large. If I were an atheist, I'd say, "How come Jesus can't keep you two together?"** ～

In fact, Satan fully intends to destroy my marriage to Carol, even though we have served side by side in the ministry for more than twenty-five years. These are the realities of spiritual warfare. Only the power of Christ can keep the two of us together as God has planned and can give us victory over Satan's destructive power. No honest minister of the gospel will deny the fact that the devil has made major assaults on his or her marriage. It's usually not talked about in public, but many tears are shed and prayers offered up to God as sincere servants of the Lord do battle against the demonic forces set on stealing their marriages, credibility, and effectiveness.

What about *our children* and *our grandchildren?* They were dedicated to God at an altar once upon a time. We stood before a minister and said with all sincerity, "O God, this baby belongs to you." But something has happened in the years since then. Now the young man or young woman is not living for God—there's no use pretending that they are.

Let's not close our eyes and make-believe otherwise. Before we can see God do what only he can do, we must spiritually diagnose exactly what is going on around us. Denying reality is not part of true Christian living.

MOST OF ALL: WHERE DID THE FAITH GO?

AT THE CORE OF ALL these losses I have mentioned is the silent theft of the most crucial element in our spiritual walk: our *faith*. What is faith? It is total dependence upon God that becomes supernatural in its working. People with faith develop a second kind of sight. They see more than just the circumstances; they see God, right beside them. Can they prove it? No. But by faith they know he's there nonetheless.

Without faith, says Hebrews 11:6, it is *impossible* to please God. Nothing else counts if faith is missing. There is no other foundation for Christian living, no matter the amount of self-effort or energy spent. Nothing else touches the Father's heart as much as when his children simply trust him wholeheartedly.

I meet people who at one time would pray over anything and everything! Even if they lost their glasses, they would pray to find them—and amazingly, the glasses would show up. Now the same people seem not to believe that God can do much of anything.

Oh, they will still give you the standard confession of faith: "Yes, I have faith in the God who answers prayer." But that vibrant trust and expectation are no more. They aren't saying, "Come on—let's go after this problem in the name of the Lord." They've been robbed.

There is an obscure story at the end of 1 Samuel that speaks to this matter in vivid detail. It is one of the low points on the roller coaster of David's life. The young conqueror of the giant Goliath is now on the run from King Saul. So many threats, so many close calls . . . he actually goes to live among the Philistines for a year, for he has run out of places to hide in Israel.

David has his own little militia of six hundred men, plus wives and children. They set up at a place called Ziklag.

When the Philistines decide to go to war against Israel, it puts David in a real crunch. He's a fighter, of course, a warrior, so he lines up with King Achish. But the Philistine generals spot him and say to their king, "What does David think he's doing?"

"Why? What do you mean?"

"The famous son-in-law of King Saul, right? No way is he going on this campaign with us!"

Achish tries to defend David's loyalty but gets nowhere. The generals say, "Look, don't you know that song they sang all over Israel? 'Saul has slain his thousands, and David his tens of thousands'—and some of those tens of thousands were us! He is definitely not going into battle with us."

So David and his militia get sent back home.

When they come close to Ziklag, they start to see smoke on the horizon. They begin a fast trot—and soon discover something dreadful: Every wife, every son, every daughter, every cow and lamb is gone. Someone has made a secret raid, burning down the city and stealing everything.

These husbands and fathers are stunned by the desolation. They are heartbroken ... imagine them thinking of their wives and daughters being captured by some roving band of marauders. *My lovely wife is missing! What is happening to my fourteen-year-old daughter right now?* They can only imagine the unrestrained brutality and heartlessness that have surely occurred. They begin to cry so hard that they run out of tears. They are devastated.

David's family is gone, too. Everything is lost.

At such a moment of human sorrow, other emotions come into play. Anger and resentment boil up. When people cannot deal with the agony of the moment, they often turn on those in authority. They can't bear the pain, so they lash out. David's men begin saying, "What were we doing out there, anyway? Whose bright idea was it to go join the Philistine army? We should have been taking care of our families. Let's stone David for this!"

Then comes this wonderful phrase in 1 Samuel 30:6: "But David found strength in the LORD his God." As the bottom was falling out of his life, he must have gone to a quiet place to pray and gather himself before God.

No matter how low you get, no matter what collapses around you, no matter who rejects you or slanders you—God is able to encourage you. He will help you get through. He will strengthen you deep within your heart in a place no one else can reach.

Having gotten back his poise, his spiritual equilibrium, David goes to the priest for a consultation with God about what he should do. Whenever David was walking in grace, he never just shot from the hip; he first sought the Lord. This is the right thing to do for anyone who is uncertain about the next move.

"Should I chase those who marauded our town, and if I do, will I find them?" he asks. A very wise question. (Think of all the terrible consequences we would avoid if we did what David did here!)

God replies, "Yes, go after them—and you will find them."

So they take off. Along the way, riding across the desert, they come upon a half-conscious Egyptian slave. After they revive him with some cool water, the man admits some vital information. "I was with the Amalekites, and we raided the area. We burned down Ziklag—but then I got sick."

"Well, how would you like to help us now—in exchange for your life?!"

The man doesn't have to think too long about that one. He agrees to guide David and his army, so they set out again.

Soon they come over the brow of a ridge to see the Amalekites below, having a big party. Drunken debauchery is the order of the day.

And in the name of the Lord, David leads his men down the hill against them. For a full twenty-four hours—all night and all the next day—they hit the Amalekites hard.

COMING BACK IN A BIG WAY

THIS WAS THE DAY that David found out that God is more than a creator. He is more than a defender. He is more than a rock or a strong tower, as David calls him in some of the Psalms. God is more than a protector from King Saul when you're hiding.

David learned the powerful truth that *God recovers stolen property*. He has a way of getting back what's been ripped off. What the enemy steals, God alone is able to recover.

And here is the best part of all: David discovered that every wife, every son, every daughter was still alive! Amazing! Not even one lamb was gone.

Listen to how the Bible describes the scene. It says that the Egyptian slave

> … led David down, and there they were, scattered over the countryside, eating, drinking and reveling because of the great amount of plunder they had taken from the land of the Philistines and from Judah. David fought them from dusk until the evening of the next day, and none of them got away, except four hundred young men who rode off on camels and fled. David recovered everything the Amalekites had taken, including his two wives. Nothing was missing: young or old, boy or girl, plunder or anything else they had taken. David brought everything back. He took all the

flocks and herds, and his men drove them ahead of the other livestock, saying, "This is David's plunder" (1 Samuel 30:16–20).

What a victory! In addition to all the recovered goods, David and his army captured an impressive amount of Amalekite goods, so that when they marched back to Ziklag, there was a *surplus*. Everyone was praising God. They were shouting, "Look what God gave us!" They came back with more than they had lost.

Why am I telling you this obscure Old Testament story? To get to this critical point: David and his men came to a moment when they chose to *get up and go after stolen property*.

The moment must come for you and me when we say, "Wait a minute—am I just going to keep sitting here feeling bad for myself? In the name of the Lord, my daughter, my son, my grandchild is going to be reclaimed. In the name of the Lord, I am *not* going to give up on my calling, my potential in life. Satan, you're going to give back that property! I come against you and resist you in the name of Jesus Christ my Lord."

Remember, we are not wrestling against flesh and blood. We are engaged in spiritual warfare. In your life and mine, here at the beginning of the twenty-first century, somebody has to step up and fight for stolen property with the weapons of faith and prayer. You have to say to the devil, "Enough! I'm going to be like David and go after the stolen goods." Get on your horse!

Our enemy Satan has no feelings of sympathy. If you don't resist, he'll rip you off every week, all year long. That's his diabolical work. But Jesus came that we might have life— abundant life. He can revive your marriage. He can bring fire back into your soul. Your spiritual calling can bloom once again.

You can recover the faith that the devil stole. I am not talking here about the mental assent you give to Bible truths you've heard over and over again. I'm talking about vibrant heart-faith and childlike trust in the risen, supernatural Christ—the kind of faith that changes the way you live, talk, and feel.

> **Here at the beginning of the twenty-first century, somebody has to step up and fight for stolen property with the weapons of faith and prayer.** ∿

Satan wants to snatch this more than anything else, for he knows "the righteous will live by faith" (Romans 1:17). He knows that "without faith it is impossible to please God" (Hebrews 11: 6). He knows that real faith is our lifeline to God's grace and power. If he can sever the *faith connection*, he has gained a tremendous victory. He knows that without a living faith, prayer as a force in our lives will be extinguished. We will soon be just mechanically going through the outward forms of religion while experiencing nothing of God's power.

But God can revive fresh faith in our souls if we ask him. He will bring faith alive in us through his Word, as Romans 10:17 declares: "Faith comes by hearing, and hearing by the word of God" (NKJV). Nothing is impossible with God. In fact, you will see God recover more than you lost, just as David did. That is what the Bible promises when it says we can be "more than conquerors through him who loved us" (Romans 8:37). The only question is, Do you and I really believe that our God will recover our stolen property? Or do we think our situation is too far gone for him?

That is why I want to tell you the story of a woman named Amalia, who had one of the most amazing recoveries I have ever seen in my life. However badly you've been plundered and ransacked in your personal life, you probably won't be able to match her traumas. But her experience will show how the power of God can turn it all around.

TWO

~

Amalia's Story

THERE'S SOMEONE WHO CAME to church the last two weeks who really needs to talk to you," Pastor Carlo Boekstaaf, my longtime associate, said one Tuesday afternoon in my office. "If it's all right, I invited her for six o'clock this evening, before the prayer meeting starts. I know a little of her story, and it's incredible. But God has definitely begun to work in her life."

Having lived my whole life in New York City and having pastored for a number of years, I figured I was beyond surprise when it came to stories from the wild side. But I must admit that what I heard that evening took my breath away. A tough-looking but attractive young woman walked into my office. She seemed to send out a strange combination of signals; while she had obviously spent time on the "mean streets," there was also a vulnerability and deep sorrow that showed through the tight-fitting clothes and heavily made-up face.

"Hi, Amalia," I said softly, motioning toward a chair. "I'm Pastor Cymbala. They said you wanted to talk to me."

She nodded slightly and sat down, tugging at her hemline.

"Tell me about yourself, if you will. How I can help you?"

In a low, husky voice she began her amazing, utterly dismal story, and for the next hour, this is essentially what I heard. . . .

I GREW UP IN THE Smith Projects on the Lower East Side.* I was the third of seven children packed into an apartment on the sixteenth floor. My father was a kitchen worker in one of the big hotels; he and my mother had both come from Puerto Rico.

The thing I remember most about our home was its fighting and arguing. We never stopped, it seemed. My father was an alcoholic and made our lives miserable. He had a wooden stick that he would swing like a crazy man at any of us who got in his way or irritated him. I never remember the family sitting down to eat a meal together. I felt very confused growing up; I mainly just tried to stay out of trouble.

My parents would argue a lot about money, since it seemed that my father never gave my mother enough to feed and clothe all us kids. Catholic Charities would help us out from time to time. Even though there wasn't enough money for the necessities, there was definitely money for alcohol. And that only made the fights worse, of course. When I would see him hitting her and pushing her around, I would just run to my room and seethe with anger.

I was about nine years old the first time I stood up to him. In the middle of the yelling, I said to him one night, "If you hurt my mother, I'm going to kill you!" How I would actually do that, I had no idea, of course; I was just upset at him.

I turned to my mother and continued, "Look—you go sleep in my bed to get away from him, and I'll sleep in yours." I thought I was helping the situation. She was really a sweet woman, and I wanted to protect her somehow.

But that was the biggest mistake of my life—because there in my parents' bedroom that night, my father began to

_____

*The Smith Projects are among the infamous public-housing high-rises that dot New York; this one sits more or less between Chinatown, Little Italy, and Wall Street in lower Manhattan.

molest me. I couldn't understand what he was doing, or why. I didn't know what to say—after all, I was just a fourth-grader.

Somehow I made it through that night, but emotionally I was a wreck.

Soon the next household fight came along—now what was I going to do? I told myself I should try again to protect my mom; maybe it would be different this time.

It was not. An ugly pattern began to be set. The only words I could find were "No, Pop, I don't want to."

"Well, if you don't," he would say, "I'm gonna beat up your mom." So I was trapped; I felt I had to go along with his wishes.

Before long, it started looking as if he was actually *starting* arguments with my mom in order to get us to switch for the night. Or he would just openly call from his room, "Come in here, Amalia. I want you in here with me." In time, I realized to my horror that I was replacing my own mother in some sick kind of way.

"Don't you ever tell your mom about this!" he would order me. "If you say a word, I'm going to kill her." The whole point of my original idea had been to somehow protect my mother, so I kept my mouth shut.

With all of this going on at home, school was an ordeal for me. I couldn't concentrate. I would be sitting in class and, instead of listening to the teacher, I'd be thinking, *Oh, no— in just another two hours I have to go home again.* I was so confused and depressed. I didn't know what to do. I didn't have a chance to grow up normally, playing with dolls and being a happy little girl. I was numb inside.

One time I got to go to a girlfriend's house after school; her name was Jeanette. To my amazement, there was no fighting in this place. It was peaceful and loving, and the family members actually listened to each other and smiled. My heart just welled up within me. *Oh, I wish I could live in a home like this!*

It was so nice being there that I stayed longer than I should have. When I realized the time and stepped outside, my mother was waiting. "Where have you been?" she asked in a worried tone. "Your father is looking for you. He's really mad!"

The minute I set foot back inside our apartment, he grabbed me and pulled me into his room. I caught such a beating that when I came out again, I was covered with blood. My mother took one look at me and immediately got me into the bathtub, where she lovingly washed the blood from my arms, legs, face, and hair.

It came to the point that when I knew I was going to have to spend the night with my father, I would hide a screw-driver or a knife under the mattress, intending to kill him. *Yes, he's my father,* I would tell myself, *but this is absolutely wrong. He is so evil that he needs to die.*

> **"Yes, he's my father, I would tell myself, *but this is absolutely wrong. He is so evil that he needs to die.*"—Amalia** ∼

When it actually came to using my weapon, though . . . I could never muster up the courage. Night after night I would go ahead and submit to him. Of all the girls in the family, I guess I was the most shy and naturally compliant. I just couldn't make myself stand up to him.

This went on for years, until I was sixteen and was eagerly plotting—like my sisters and brothers—to get out of the house as soon as possible. For me, the escape route was a boy named Richard, who lived in the building across from us and was in my grade in school. We started hanging out together—much to my father's displeasure. The only way I knew to get Richard to accept me and love me was to give him my body. Wasn't that what all men wanted?

We soon found a minister to marry us and had a big Puerto Rican reception in the community center of our project. I don't recall that my father even attended; he was always hostile to any of my boyfriends, and certainly my new husband.

We couldn't afford a honeymoon; we just moved into a house a distant relative let us use. This was basically the end of schooling for me. Richard had a job at Metropolitan Hospital, and I figured he would take care of me from now on; I didn't really need to finish high school. Any dreams of what I myself might accomplish in life were left to fade away.

It was hard to have a normal sexual relationship with my teenage husband. Intimacy of any kind always got me thinking about my father again. Our marriage never really had a chance.

Meanwhile, Richard introduced me to drugs, starting with pot. At first I didn't like it, but he kept coaxing me along, and soon I realized it could make me forget all my problems at least for a while. Then came LSD and cocaine. I tried shooting up with some heroin, too—but I didn't like it, because it was a downer. I wanted anything I took to lift me up and make me happy.

The marriage lasted little more than a year. I found myself intrigued with other men, and some women as well. Richard and I split up, and he soon headed off to the army. Meanwhile, I got involved with one man after another, trying to stay high twenty-four hours a day. I got odd jobs as necessary—a shoe factory, a donut shop, whatever I could find with my limited education. But any man who would offer me some sweet talk and a place to stay could have me. And if he would provide drugs as well, so much the better.

I wore crazy outfits to catch attention on the street. I got a sales job at a pretty wild boutique called "Superfly" on Forty-Seventh and Broadway, which kept me up on all the latest fashion. Somehow I earned a reputation for dating boxers. One night I was in an underground disco when a world-famous boxing champion came in. His friend dared me to go ask him for a dance, and I did. By the end of the evening, he had invited me to his hotel.

I was with another guy that particular evening, so I turned the champ down. But a few days later, he showed up in my store, drawing a big crowd of fans on the street. He came around not so much to shop as to ask me out to dinner, and I accepted. That night, after we had been seated at our table in a fancy restaurant, he said, "Here's a pill for you. Take it—it'll make you feel good."

"What is it?" I asked.

"Just trust me. You'll like it," he said.

Whatever he hoped it would do to me—it had the opposite effect. Within minutes I was in the ladies' room throwing up! All through the meal I felt awful. Afterward he took me to his hotel room, but there definitely wasn't going to be any "action" that night—I was too sick to my stomach. I finally told him I really needed to just take a taxi home. I asked him for some cash; he was so disgusted with me that he refused. So I had to pay my own fare.

Another guy I dated in those days was actually a pimp, although I didn't realize it. When we were out, he would park his Cadillac along West Forty-Second Street and watch certain prostitutes, leaving me to wonder, *Why? Isn't he interested in me?* I didn't get it: Those were his girls! Only when he tried to put me into his business, too, did I wake up and stop seeing him.

I was now in my mid-twenties, and all this fast living just wasn't as great as I thought it would be, you know? I decided that maybe I should get a steady line of work. So I signed up to take a bartending course. Why, I don't know, because I hated all alcoholics.

When I finished the course and got my certificate, I had trouble finding a job. A lot of places in those days still weren't too open to the idea of women bartenders. When I applied at a place in Midtown called "Metropole," they said no but offered to hire me as a barmaid instead. With my low self-confidence, I said okay, I'd take the job.

Not until I reported for work did I realize what the tiny stage in the center of the bar was for. This was in fact a top-less go-go bar. *Now what have I gotten myself into?* I said. But a job was a job—and I definitely needed one, so I went to work.

The men who would come there were friendly to me, and sometimes they'd say things like, "Hey, why don't you go up there, too?"

I would glance at the girls on stage ... and soon I came to realize that that's where the real money was. Here I was, slaving away for $200 a week plus tips, while they got paid a regular salary plus all the twenty- and fifty-dollar bills that customers would tuck into their costumes when they danced. I was afraid ...but after a while, as the encouragements kept coming, I got the bar owner to switch my job.

My first time on stage was nerve-wracking. In fact, I probably couldn't have done it if I hadn't gotten high to start with. But as minutes went by and the customers started cheering and throwing money my way, I saw the benefits of this line of work.

... And that's what I've been doing for the past four years. I'm not wild about it—but what else am I going to do? Sometimes I think to myself, *How did I ever get into all this? I'm degrading myself. This isn't what I really want to do.* I get depressed and just think there's nothing else. My father already destroyed everything I once dreamed of being. I don't care how far I go now ... but then again, I do care, you know?

My finances really took a hit a couple of years ago as the result of meeting this man named Gilbert at the Metropole. I was attracted to him. We started dating. And then one night, right in the middle of a dance, I passed out—collapsed right there on stage.

I figured I had had too many Black Russian drinks that night. But the real cause was, I was pregnant. I'd been pregnant before, several times, and had always just gotten abortions so I could keep working. But this time it was different. For some reason, I wanted to go ahead and see what having a baby would be like.

> **"I'd been pregnant before, several times, and had always just gotten abortions. But this time, for some reason, I wanted to see what having a baby would be like."—Amalia ～**

Gilbert wasn't interested in sticking around for that, though, and promptly took off. I was devastated. I was left all alone—and unable to work due to the pregnancy. Eventually the electricity was cut off because I wasn't able to pay the bill. I really hit bottom. I decided it would probably be best if I just killed myself, either by slashing my wrists or else jumping off a bridge. I took a blade and started making a line on my wrist. I began to bleed. But I couldn't bring myself to cut deep enough to finish the job.

I had to humble myself and ask my mother if I could move back home. (My dad had left her by this time—the police had been called to restrain him so many times that he finally decided he'd better get out of New York City.) She took me in. I admit that I dumped a lot of anger on her. She asked me one day why I couldn't seem to finish a single sentence without using a four-letter word. We got into a big fight. Underneath, I think I was still mad at her for what happened years before.

In time, I gave birth to a healthy baby boy, whom I named Vinny. This was the most beautiful experience of my life. When I looked at him in my arms, I couldn't help feeling grateful to God.

Now I'm asking myself, how am I going to bring him up? What am I going to teach him? I don't know. . . .

In order to support him, I've had to go back to my old work. My mother takes care of the baby while I'm gone each day.

Once, after another argument with my mother, I went up on the roof of our building. Looking down eighteen stories toward the street below, I thought about the lousy job of mothering I was doing—coming home stoned at three in the morning and making my mother do all the real work. Maybe I should just jump. I began shaking and crying.

Somehow I pulled myself away, went downstairs, and went to sit in the quietness of the Catholic church my mother attends. I kept shaking and crying as I said, "God, why am I going through all this? How come you let my life get so out of control? It's all your fault."

Then my latest lover broke off our relationship, and I was devastated and even more confused. I got really serious about making a definite plan for suicide; I would go on one of the bridges and jump into the East River. I was scared to do it, but I was more scared to go on living.

My sister's husband, whose name is Mickey, has done plenty of partying with me in the past. But now he has become a Christian. So has a friend named Carmen. Suddenly she's not interested in getting high with me; now she keeps talking to me about Jesus.

So a couple of weeks ago, Mickey invited my mother and some of the rest of us to come with him here to your church. "All right, I'll go," I said.

We sat in the balcony. I probably wasn't dressed right for church, but—whatever. Mickey seemed so happy, sitting there with a big smile on his face. I couldn't figure out why.

When you got up there to preach and started to speak about God's love, I listened. I remember you saying something about "Jesus loves you no matter what you've done. He will forgive you and take you past whatever has been done to you in your life."

Pretty soon I was going, *How does he know what I'm going through? Did Mickey tell him about my life, or what?* I couldn't believe that God really understood my crazy life. All kinds of questions came to my mind.

Then, without warning, I started to cry. That's not me— I'm pretty tough. But I couldn't hold back the tears. It was ruining my makeup.

When you asked people to come to the front for prayer, I got up and went with the rest. A woman came along and laid her hand on my shoulder. That kind of spooked me— I'm not used to anything like that. But all she was doing was praying for me.

When I went home, I kept thinking about it all. I was still confused about some things. The next day, one of your pastors called to thank me for coming and to ask me how I was doing. At the end, he said, "Are you ready to trust Christ with your life?"

"Well, I don't think I'm ready for that," I answered. After all, I used to laugh at Christian television programs when I'd get high on LSD. But something was happening inside of me. I decided I should come back to your church and at least find out if I'd been "set up," if you all had some kind of plan to get to me.

So I came back this past Sunday. Your message was about the peace of God.

That same pastor caught me again and asked if I wanted to speak to you. I tried to act cool and said, "Well, why should I?" But inside, I knew I needed to.

I looked at this poor woman, so ravaged by sin and Satan, and my heart just broke. She turned to me as if to say, *What next? Am I hopeless?* ~

If something doesn't change soon, then—Pastor, I'm really messed up. I'll be honest with you—I feel really dirty even being here in your office. I don't know if I should have told you all this, but . . . anyway . . . um, maybe I should stop talking now. . . .

~

THE TEARS HAD BEEN welling up in my eyes as Amalia told her story. A knot in my throat kept me from speaking. We sat there in the silence, both of us thinking deeply. It seemed to me that she had already lived three or four lives—all of them incredibly horrible.

I looked at this poor woman, so ravaged by sin and Satan, and my heart just broke. She turned to me as if to say,

What next? Am I hopeless? Do you want to just kick me out into the street, or what?

I glanced at the clock and realized the prayer meeting would soon be starting. Suddenly, I knew exactly what to do.

"Amalia," I said, "we're going to go into the prayer meeting now and ask God to do a miracle. Jesus Christ can cleanse you and make you into the woman he wants you to be. He brought you here so we could tell you the way out of the mess you're in.

"If you want Christ to save and change you, then come with me right now, and I'll have the whole church pray for you."

She kind of nodded, and we left my office. We walked down the center aisle of the church as people were already praying all around us. We sat down in the front pew.

Later, I took the microphone and announced that God had sent a special visitor to us that night. Soon Amalia was standing in front of the whole congregation. I told them none of her story—only that she had come to a crisis in her life and wanted to receive Christ as Savior. What a wonderful time we had as we prayed together and then worshiped "the Father of compassion and the God of all comfort" (2 Corinthians 1:3)!

Amalia told me later that when she went home that night to her mother, who was baby-sitting young Vinny, she exclaimed, "Mom, guess what I did tonight! I gave my heart to Jesus Christ, and he saved me! He cleansed me! I'm not the same anymore."

Her mother was speechless. Was this troubled daughter of hers finally going to straighten out?

"That night was the best sleep I'd ever had," Amalia reported, "because I felt clean. Jesus did it! No more nightmares, no more drugs, no more self-hatred, no more despair."

Pastor Boekstaaf and his wife, Ingrid, got Amalia into a Monday night discipleship group in their home. We began to see a transformation in her life. She began to look different. Her eyes brightened. Her wardrobe changed. She began to carry herself like a godly young woman instead of what sin had made her become. She found a job as a receptionist in a small law firm, then moved on to a Wall Street insurance company.

Eventually Amalia joined the Brooklyn Tabernacle Choir. A year or two later, when we held a big public concert at Radio City Music Hall, we asked her to share her testimony just before a song my wife, Carol, wrote entitled, "I'm Clean!" After her story, the choir began to sing:

> There is a blood, a cleansing blood that flows
>   from Calvary,
> And in this blood, there's a saving power,
> For it washed me white and made me clean....
> Oh, I stand today with my heart so clean;
> Through the blood that Jesus shed I'm truly free.

While the choir sang, we showed a series of slides on the big screen—one picture after another that Amalia had loaned us. The hardness and degradation kept building until finally the frame dissolved slowly into the beautiful woman she had now become, in a sequined white choir gown. It seemed that all six thousand people broke down in tears together.

A few years after her salvation, Amalia met a dental technician in our church, and they fell in love and were married. The Lord gave them a son together, a half brother to Vinny, and the family moved in 1987 to another state. There they continue today to walk with God, worshiping and serving in a church pastored by a good friend of mine.

I have told Amalia's story at some length here to make the point that no matter how thoroughly the devil messes up a life—no matter how early in childhood he starts, and how frightfully he corrupts the human soul—God can take back this stolen property.

If God could change Amalia, then what are you facing that is "too impossible" for him? If God responded to her cry for mercy and grace, what is stopping you from calling on the Lord right now? God invites you to do that, and there is no better time than today. Listen to his loving invitation: "Call upon me in the day of trouble; I *will* deliver you, and you will honor me" (Psalm 50:15).

> **No matter how thoroughly the devil messes up a life—no matter how early in childhood he starts—God can take back this stolen property.** ∾

You can see Jesus Christ prove himself more powerful than the thief who steals. This very moment is crucial, even as you read these words. Face the reality of your spiritual situation, and go after anything God has shown you to be stolen property that Satan has cleverly taken from you. The zeal and love for Christ you once had *can* be recovered. The calling on your life to serve the Lord in a particular ministry can still be fulfilled.

It's not too late, either, for God to reach that son and daughter, no matter where they are or how they seem to be doing. The family that is falling apart right now is not too hard a case for Jesus Christ if you will just stand and begin to ask in faith that he restore what the thief has tried to steal. God will do it, and you will praise him in a new way.

THREE

~

The Question Nobody Is Asking

When most of us think about how we are doing spiritually, we think about surface things. We zero in on behavior patterns, such as have we been gossiping, have we been staying true to our marriage, have we been reading our Bibles, have we been tithing? We concentrate on outward works while forgetting that they are simply the fruit of a deeper spiritual factor.

In the organized church, too many pastors are interested in attendance alone, which has nothing to do with a church's health. What matters is not how many people are showing up, but how active and vibrant their faith is in the God they serve. You can easily pack a building without pleasing God, because crowds do not equal spirituality.

When Paul sent Timothy to check up on the new Thessalonian church (where he had been able to spend only three weeks before getting run out of town), you think he would have asked first about the church's growth. Did they have a building of their own yet? How many people were attending on Sundays? Were the offerings enough to cover the bills? And what about the individual people: Had they stopped swearing, drinking, carousing? Going to see bad entertainment? Sleeping around?

Not at all! Instead, in 1 Thessalonians 3, the apostle Paul reveals that his primary concern is for the *faith level* of his precious converts. He wants to take a temperature reading of their spiritual health, and faith is what he is looking for. He doesn't just assume that because they are Christians, they are automatically walking in robust faith. Listen to his words and see how unfamiliar his approach is to our modern ears:

- "We sent Timothy . . . to strengthen and encourage you in *your faith*" (v. 2).
- "When I could stand it no longer, I sent to find out about *your faith*" (v. 5).
- "But Timothy has just now come to us from you and has brought good news about *your faith* and love" (v. 6).
- "Therefore, brothers, in all our distress and persecution we were encouraged about you because of *your faith*" (v. 7).
- "Night and day we pray most earnestly that we may see you again and supply what is lacking in *your faith*" (v. 10).

From top to bottom throughout this chapter, Paul is churned up about one simple word. In fact, this is more than a checkup, an inspection. He has sent Timothy to "strengthen and encourage" the people in their faith—in other words, to do what he could to make the report better.

Timothy has brought back a great summary, as quoted above. Nothing is said about the Thessalonian building, you notice. Nothing about the sound system or the lights or the carpet. Instead, a lot of attention to their faith. But even that isn't enough for Paul. In verse 10 he says he wants to make another trip there himself to "see you again and supply what is lacking in your faith." Faith. Faith. Faith. Faith.

Why this emphasis?

WHAT MOVES THE HEART OF GOD

WHAT PAUL KNEW, but what we seem to have forgotten, is that when people break down in their behavior, backslide into sinful living, or grow cold in the Lord, it is because their faith has broken down first. When someone's temper keeps flaring out of control, that is not the real problem; down underneath is a weakness of faith. So it is with all our departures from right living.

My ministry goal in the Brooklyn Tabernacle is not to fill the building. It is to preach the Word of God in such a way that people's faith in Christ is built up. God doesn't need the beautiful music of a church choir. If he wanted great music, he'd have the angels sing! They never miss a word or sing off-key. But what he is really after is a people who show a strong, personal faith in him.

> **God doesn't need the beautiful music of a church choir. If he wanted great music, he'd have the angels sing!** ~

What do you think it would take to amaze Jesus? After all, through him the world and all humanity were created in the first place. He has forever existed in heaven itself. While on earth, was there anything that impressed him to the point of exclaiming, "That's really something! Wow!" Never in any chapter of the four Gospels was Jesus astounded by anybody's righteousness. After all, he was entirely pure and holy himself. Never was he impressed with anyone's wisdom or education. Never did he say, "Boy, Matthew sure is smart, isn't he? I really picked out a financial genius there."

But he *was* amazed by one thing: people's faith.

When he told the Roman centurion he would go to his house to heal his servant, and the centurion said not to bother but just to speak the word of healing, Jesus "was amazed at him, and turning to the crowd following him, he said, 'I tell you, I have not found such *great faith* even in Israel'" (Luke 7:9). The Jewish listeners probably didn't appreciate being outclassed by this Roman, but that is the way it happened, regardless.

> **Never in the four Gospels was Jesus astounded by anybody's righteousness. Never was he impressed with anyone's education. But he *was* amazed by one thing: people's faith.** ～

When another "foreigner," a Canaanite woman, came pleading on behalf of her demon-possessed daughter and wouldn't take no for an answer, Jesus exclaimed at last, "Woman, you have *great faith!* Your request is granted" (Matthew 15:28).

On the other hand, when he went back to his hometown of Nazareth, where he had grown up, "he could not do any miracles there, except lay his hands on a few sick people and heal them. And he was amazed at their *lack of faith*" (Mark 6:5–6). You can be sure that no sickness was too extreme, no demon too powerful for the Son of the living God. But on that particular day in Nazareth, his hands were tied by their unbelief. In fact, he laid down this statement as a first principle: "According to your faith will it be done to you" (Matthew 9:29).

We can't twist the story theologically by saying, "Well, maybe it wasn't God's will for him to heal those folks in

Nazareth." The text gives no indication of that. It clearly says the Son of God was limited that day.

Faith alone is the trigger that releases divine power. As Peter wrote, it is "through *faith* [that we] are shielded by God's power" (1 Peter 1:5). Our trying, struggling, or promising won't work—faith is what God is after. Faith is the key to our relationship with him.

MORE THAN TALK

I AM NOT JUST talking about our words. Faith is far more than talk. Sometimes we are not much better than those in Isaiah's time, of whom the Lord said, "These people come near to me with their mouth and honor me with their lips, but their hearts are far from me" (Isaiah 29:13).

> **In our time, the whole notion of faith has been derailed in some quarters into an emphasis on saying certain words, giving a "positive confession" of health, prosperity, or other blessings.** ~

In our time, the whole notion of faith has been derailed in some quarters into an emphasis on saying certain words, giving a "positive confession," or announcing a superconfident description of health, prosperity, or other blessings. You know, a kind of spiritual mantra. A mental formula of "how the Bible will work for you" is front and center, while the question of a true heart-faith and communion with the living Christ is rarely emphasized.

This formula is not the spirit or message of the New Testament, and it leads to gross absurdities. It actually has dampened the desire for real prayer meetings all across the land. People cannot call out to the Lord for answers to their problems because, according to their teaching, you shouldn't even say you have a problem. To admit that you're sick or in trouble is supposedly bad; you're using your mouth to say something negative, and that is not "living in faith."

If that is true, why did the apostle James declare, "Is any one of you in trouble? He should pray. . . . Is any one of you sick? He should call the elders of the church to pray over him and anoint him with oil in the name of the Lord" (James 5:13–14). How can we truly pray, or ask others to pray, unless we first admit we're facing some kind of real problem? Believers in the New Testament obviously did this.

A minister once told me that when people come to the altar in his church for individual prayer, he has trained them not to say, "I have a cold" or "I have diabetes" or whatever. Instead, they are to say, "I have *the symptoms of* a cold" or "I have *the symptoms of* diabetes." Otherwise, they would not be walking "in faith." (I guess when someone has stopped breathing for two weeks, they have only "the symptoms of death.")

To me, this is little more than a mind game. The faith God wants for us does not shrink from facing the reality of the problem head-on. When Abraham saw the years going by without a child coming into his home, he didn't say, "My wife and I seem to be having some of the symptoms of infertility." Instead, he was totally straightforward: *"Without weakening in his faith,* he faced the fact that his body was as good as dead— since he was about a hundred years old—and that Sarah's womb was also dead. Yet he did not waver through unbelief regarding the promise of God, but *was strengthened in his faith* and gave glory to God, being fully persuaded that God had power to do what he had promised" (Romans 4:19–21).

Isn't that a powerful Scripture? Realism about the problem was not anti-faith in the slightest. In fact, it made Abraham say, "O God, you are the only one who can change this situation. Come and help us, we pray!"

Paul and the other biblical writers were not promoting "fantasy faith" or "hyper-faith." Nothing in 1 Thessalonians 3 even seems to touch on how the Christians in that city talked or what kind of declarations they made. Paul was looking for something far deeper: true faith.

STRUGGLE ON AND ON?

BY CONTRAST, THERE ARE many others going to church today in America whose faith has gone dormant. They would never admit that, of course. They would claim to have faith in God and his Word. They stand in church on Sunday morning and recite the Apostles' Creed.

But if you watch carefully, you will see a hybrid Christianity. You will see people who think that the object of Christianity is to read the Bible every day, try to live a good life as best they can, and thus earn God's approval.

> **Whatever happened to the core truth of the Protestant Reformation, namely, that we do not earn our way with God but rather receive his grace by faith?** ~

Their key word in describing the Christian life is "struggle." They say things such as "I'm *struggling* to obey the Lord and do his will. I'm doing the best I can. We all *struggle*, you know." What this reveals is a Christianity focused on our ability rather than God's.

Whatever happened to the core truth of the Protestant Reformation, namely, that we do not earn our way with God but rather receive his grace by faith? Like the Galatians, we have walked away from something vital. No wonder the apostle Paul sent them a stern letter that said, "Are you so foolish? After beginning with the Spirit, are you now trying to attain your goal by human effort?" (Galatians 3:3).

True Christianity is, rather, to know Jesus and trust in him, to rely on him, to admit that all of our strength comes from him. That kind of faith is not only what pleases God, but is also the only channel through which the power of God flows into our lives so we *can* live victoriously for him. It is what Paul meant when he wrote, "I can do everything *through him [Christ] who gives me strength*" (Philippians 4:13).

My coauthor, Dean Merrill, was at a wedding recently in which the bride and groom's responses to the vows were not just the traditional "I do" but rather "I will, with the help of God." The minister who wrote that ceremony knew that human effort alone might not carry the young couple in today's world "until death do you part." He therefore called on them to implore the help of God in building their marriage.

> When most people break down in their Christian life, they simply "try harder." Lots of luck! Try harder with what? ～

This declaration was very much in keeping with what Solomon said at the dedication of the Temple: "May the LORD our God be with us as he was with our fathers; may he never leave us nor forsake us. *May he turn our hearts to him*, to walk in all his ways and to keep the commands, decrees and regulations he gave our fathers" (1 Kings 8:57–58). In that sentence Solomon showed great insight into the fact that God himself must turn our hearts toward him, or else we will stray.

When most people break down in their Christian life, they simply "try harder." Lots of luck! Try harder with what? I've looked inside of me—and stopped looking. There's nothing in there that's good or usable. On the other hand, if I turn the other way and begin "looking unto Jesus, the author and finisher of our faith" (Hebrews 12:2 KJV), I find everything I need.

It does no good to try to control people and get them to behave by giving them only laws and threats about hell. That won't cut it. They won't change. How do the righteous actually live? "By faith."

> **The greatest Christian is not the one who has *achieved* the most but rather the one who has *received* the most.** ~

When I was growing up, I thought the greatest Christian must be the person who walks around with shoulders thrown back because of tremendous inner strength and power, quoting Scripture and letting everyone know he has arrived. I have since learned that the most mature believer is the one who is bent over, leaning most heavily on the Lord, and admitting his total inability to do anything without Christ. The greatest Christian is not the one who has *achieved* the most but rather the one who has *received* the most. God's grace, love, and mercy flow through him abundantly because he walks in total dependence.

I remember an afternoon many years ago when God made this truth come alive in my heart. While driving down a New Jersey boulevard, I was listening to an elderly minister from Great Britain whose books had blessed me as a young pastor. The radio station was broadcasting a tape of one of his last messages preached at a well-known Bible conference here in America.

The speaker related how, after many years of successful ministry as a teacher and expositor of God's Word, he was forced to stay home due to a lingering illness. This change from his usual busy schedule of speaking, traveling, and writing began to slowly bring on a sense of depression. He struggled to overcome it by fastening his attention on God's Word, but that was difficult due to his ill health.

"Suddenly," he related, "it seemed as if a sewer top had been lifted, and an ugly host of temptations, irritations, and evil thoughts rose up to besiege me." Here he was, a noted Bible teacher and author, fighting against things he had not encountered for many years. His voice broke slightly as he shared his horror at being tempted even to swear, something that had never surfaced in his entire life, even before he became a Christian.

"How can this be?" he cried to the Lord. "After all these years of Christian service and careful study of the Bible, why am I in such a desperate battle?"

As he sought the Lord, God made real to him that his human nature had never really changed. Oh, yes, "if anyone is in Christ, he is a new creation" (2 Corinthians 5:17)—but only because *Christ* is in him as the indwelling Savior and Helper.

I pulled over to the curb that afternoon and wept. One of my heroes in the faith had stunned me with his vulnerability. In the same way, I had to admit that Jim Cymbala the man had never changed—the "old man," the flesh, my sinful nature. Apart from God's grace and power, I too was hopeless.

The truth is that God never works with our "flesh," or old nature—that's how depraved it is. That is why we never stop needing the power of the Holy Spirit during our whole pilgrimage here on earth. We never reach a place where we can live victoriously apart from his daily grace in our lives. Only the Spirit can produce *his* fruit, in and through us, that makes us the people God wants us to be. And God has to show us regularly how needy we are.

The great apostle Paul himself had to learn that seeming contradiction of God's strength coming out of personal weakness. He writes in 2 Corinthians 12:9–10 that the Lord "said to me, 'My grace is sufficient for you, for my power is made perfect in weakness.' Therefore I will boast all the more gladly about my weaknesses, so that Christ's power may rest on me. That is why, for Christ's sake, I delight in weaknesses, in insults, in hardships, in persecutions, in difficulties. For when I am weak, then I am strong."

Paul is not just trying to be overly humble or self-deprecating here. He has found the secret that we were created to be receiving vessels only—not having any strength in ourselves but merely depending on God to fill us hourly with all we need. Paul also knew that God uses trouble and trials of all kinds to heighten that sensitivity so that by faith we can use divine resources.

Don't give up today because you feel weak and overwhelmed—that's the very place where divine power will uphold you if you only believe and call out to the Lord in total dependence. Childlike faith in God is not only what pleases him but is also the secret of our strength and power.

"HELP, LORD!"

IF WE ONLY ATTACK the symptoms of unbelief—the various outbreaks of sin in our churches, for example—we will never get to the root cause. That is why legalistic preaching never produces true spirituality. It might seem to do so for the moment, but it cannot last. Christians become strong only by seeing and understanding the grace of God, which is received by faith.

> **If we only attack the symptoms of unbelief—
> the various outbreaks of sin—we will never
> get to the root cause. Legalistic preaching
> never produces true spirituality. ～**

Some years ago I was taking my granddaughter Susie on a walk when a couple of homeless men came walking toward us. Their scruffy appearance made her afraid. In her little mind, she thought she was about to be harmed. She was already holding my hand, but instantly I felt her push her body into mine as she grabbed onto my pant leg. "Papa!" she whispered. Of course, I put my arm around her and said that everything was going to be all right. The men passed us on the sidewalk without incident.

Inside, my heart was brimming. That instantaneous reflex of reaching out for my aid meant that she thought I could handle anything and everything. This was a more precious gift than any sweater she would ever give me for Christmas. She showed that she had a deep faith in me. I would come to her rescue. I would meet her urgent need. I would take care of her.

That is the very thing that delights the heart of God. When we run to him and throw ourselves upon him in believing prayer, he rejoices. He does not want me out on my own, trying to earn merit stars from him. He wants us, rather, to lean into him, walking with him as closely as possible. He is not so much interested in our *doing* as in our *receiving* from him. After all, what can we do or say or conquer without first receiving grace at God's throne to help us in our time of need (Hebrews 4:16)? And all that receiving happens through faith.

Possibly there is a need in your life today to stop all the struggling with your own strength. Let it go, and call out to God in simple faith. Remember that no one has ever been disappointed after putting trust in him. Not one person throughout all of human history has ever depended upon God and found that God let him down. Never! Not once!

Face the obvious fact that the problem or need is far too big for you to handle. Use the very fact of your inadequacy as a springboard to a new, wholehearted trust in God's unfailing promises.

> Therefore let everyone who is godly pray to you
>   while you may be found;
> surely when the mighty waters rise,
>   they will not reach him.
> You are my hiding place;
>   you will protect me from trouble
>   and surround me with songs of deliverance. *Selah*
>
> I will instruct you and teach you in the way you
>   should go;
>   I will counsel you and watch over you.
> Do not be like the horse or the mule,
>   which have no understanding
> but must be controlled by bit and bridle
>   or they will not come to you.
> Many are the woes of the wicked,
>   but the LORD's unfailing love
>   surrounds the man who trusts in him.
>
> Rejoice in the LORD and be glad, you righteous;
>   sing, all you who are upright in heart!
>   (Psalm 32:6–11)

PART 2

~

Getting Past
the Barricades

FOUR

~

Free from a
Hurtful Past

Aʟʟ ᴛʜɪs ᴛᴀʟᴋ ᴀʙᴏᴜᴛ faith and God's promises is wonderful, but I've learned that it sometimes falls on deaf ears. Many people carry scars from days gone by. Life has not been kind to them. The idea that God might act powerfully on their behalf strikes them right away as too good to be true. *Maybe somebody else, but not me. Others can get answers to their prayers, but not me. Nothing much can change my life now. Too much has happened, too much has already gone wrong....*

Whenever I meet this kind of person, I always think about a special secret in the life of Joseph. Even if the person has heard his story before, I go through it again, telling how Joseph grew up in what we would call a classic "dysfunctional family." Most circumstances in his boyhood years were beyond his control. After all, he was the eleventh son out of twelve—far down the line.

Joseph's father, Jacob, favors him. For some reason, something about Joseph strikes a tender cord inside of Jacob. The boy has come along late in his life and is the firstborn son of his beloved wife, Rachel.

All this attention turns out to be a curse for Joseph instead of a blessing. The special coat he receives from his father makes him a marked young man. The more Jacob does for him, the more his older brothers hate him. (Siblings have a way of picking up on any little inequity; they notice it right away, and they resent it.)

When Joseph is seventeen years old, he tattles on some of his brothers about something they have done out in the field (see Genesis 37:2). This obviously does not improve the situation. Nobody likes a snitch, especially if he's the father's pet.

On top of all this, God begins to give Joseph dreams about the future. Joseph hasn't asked for this; it just happens. In his youthfulness, he makes the mistake of talking about his dreams—the sheaves of grain that all bow down to his sheaf, and the sun, moon, and stars that bow down to him. With this last one, even his father gets upset. "Get a grip, son!" says Jacob (I'm paraphrasing here). "What are you trying to say— that you're going to run the whole family? That your mother and I and all your brothers are going to bow down to you?"

"I don't know what it means, Dad. I'm just telling you what I saw."

Obviously, this family is not functioning smoothly. For all of us who had rough moments growing up, for all of us who have ever been hurt by a family member, we can understand. Joseph's brothers can see no good in him and never say even one kind word. All of this is taking a toll on Joseph's tender heart.

The Plot Thickens

Joseph is sent one day to see how his brothers are getting along with the sheep in the open fields. After a couple of stops, he finds them near Dothan. As he is coming toward them, they look up and see that colorful coat. "Here comes Daddy's boy," someone snarls. Anger boils up anew.

They are all alone on the wide plains. This is a perfect setting for revenge, and a plan takes shape in a matter of minutes. They will not just ignore him, curse him, or even hit him—this time, *they will kill him.*

Within seconds, they grab him and rip off the hated coat. Joseph, being in his late teens, no doubt puts up a vigorous fight. He struggles, but in vain; clearly outnumbered, he is mauled. Several of them intend to kill him immediately, but Reuben, the oldest, suggests shoving him into a cistern, a deep pit in the ground that retains water. Quickly he goes sliding down into the mud hole, his heart pounding with panic, feeling their hatred up close.

Joseph, a sensitive young man, could actually hear his own brothers talk about murdering him. Imagine the emotional trauma of crouching there, helpless, and listening to this from your own siblings. What a jolt to his young mind and heart!

Meanwhile, his brothers coldly sit down to have lunch (Genesis 37:25).

While they are eating, a trading caravan comes along. Older brother Judah suddenly gets a bright idea. "Look, guys, it will be less messy if, instead of killing him, we just sell him as a slave to these traders. That way we can make a little profit on the deal."

Imagine Joseph being pulled back up out of the pit by his brothers, his clothing a muddy mess, if not already torn off. See his eyes wide with shock as his brothers haggle with the traders: "Good-looking kid, don't you think? How much will you pay for him? Only twelve shekels? Ah, come on—he's worth more than that! Twenty-five at least."

Joseph is numb by now. His own brothers are selling him down the river. The bargaining continues. Finally, they settle on twenty shekels. "Sold!"

He watches the silver pieces being counted. Tears well up in his eyes. This can't really be happening, can it? He won't be going back home. Strangers grab him roughly, treat him like a piece of meat, and thrust him toward their caravan.

(It's a good thing Joseph didn't know what his brothers said when they returned home to Jacob: "Look, Dad!—we found Joseph's coat with all this blood on it. It looks like something terrible has happened." And when their father collapsed in tears of grief, they had the gall to pretend to mourn along with him. "God be with you, Dad. It's hard, we know! He was a wonderful brother...." What a charming group of young men.)

A FUTURE AFTER ALL?

BUT THE BIBLE SAYS in Genesis 39:2 that "the LORD was with Joseph." Somehow, standing there on the block in the Egyptian slave market, Joseph ends up getting purchased by Potiphar, a man of prestige and wealth.

An odd thing begins to happen as the weeks and months go by. His master notices that whatever Joseph touches seems to prosper. Potiphar realizes he can trust his young Hebrew slave and gradually gives him more responsibility. In time, he makes him the general manager of his household.

The only trouble is, Potiphar's wife is apparently having other thoughts about Joseph, who is a little too young and handsome for her to ignore. She begins to make a move on him. He turns her down, but she is not easily dissuaded. She keeps flirting with him, until the day comes when her husband is at work, and nobody else is around—just the two of them. Suddenly she reaches for him, grabbing his coat and insisting that he yield to her desires.

But Joseph does not want to disgrace either God or Potiphar, his master, by giving in to this woman. If he loses God's approval, he will lose everything valuable in life. He quickly wrestles his way out of his coat and runs for the exits.

(Funny how Joseph seems to keep having trouble with coats, isn't it?)

Potiphar's wife, humiliated, immediately begins to scream, "Rape! Rape!" The other servants come rushing in, and by that evening Potiphar has heard her whole twisted version of the story. The next day, Joseph's life comes crashing down for the second time. He is promptly arrested and ends up in the slammer.

What is he thinking now? *How could this happen? Why?!* Yet, even in prison, God is with Joseph. His talent and honesty rise like cream to the top. The warden begins to notice the same characteristics that had originally caught Potiphar's attention. Before long, Joseph is put in charge of his cell block. The place is not as plush as Potiphar's house, to be sure, but at least he has some room to maneuver.

Months go by. Joseph lies awake every night thinking about all that has happened to him. The disaster that day in the open field outside Dothan ... the caravan ride to Egypt ... the hopes that got dashed while working for Potiphar. Now he's a convict. His family has no idea where he is, and most of them don't care. There is no legal statute to appeal to, no court-appointed attorney. Where is God in all of this? How will those dreams ever come true?

Joseph lies awake every night thinking about all that has happened to him. Where is God in all of this? ~

One day a couple of new prisoners show up. Pharaoh has gotten irritated with his baker and his cupbearer, the fellow who had the lucky job of tasting all Pharaoh's wine ahead of time to be sure it wasn't poisoned. (What a great way to make a living!) On the same night both of these prisoners have dreams. The baker's has to do with bakery goods, and the cupbearer's has to do with wine. Both suspect that the dreams have significance, but they can't figure them out.

Joseph then steps in with interpretations from God— one of them a disastrous outcome, the other a happy one. And his predictions come true.

As the cupbearer is dancing out the door to freedom, Joseph says, "Please, friend . . . remember me when you get out of this place, okay? I'm doing time for no crime at all. I really don't deserve to be here."

"Sure. Don't worry—you can count on me."

Joseph's heart skips a beat with anticipation. Maybe this will be his big break.

MORE DARKNESS

BUT UNBELIEVABLY, THE CUPBEARER somehow "forgets." And for two more needless years, Joseph rots in his cell.

And we think we have problems? People have forgotten to appreciate us? How would you like to help somebody and have that person promptly forget that you even exist?

After two years, God steps in to overrule human frailty. This time, a vivid dream comes to Pharaoh himself. In fact, it is a "double feature." First he sees seven fats cows coming out of the Nile followed by seven skinny cows, which swallow the fat ones. Then he sees approximately the same thing again, only with heads of grain.

He calls for Egypt's best magicians and occultists—a specialty in Egyptian culture—and asks for the interpretation of what he has dreamed. They are completely baffled.

Off in one corner, the cupbearer is muttering to himself, "Dreams . . . dreams . . . oh, now I remember! Pharaoh!

There's a young Hebrew in prison I totally forgot about. He's amazing at dream interpretation."

And that is how Joseph ends up before the imperial throne, saying, "I cannot do it, . . . but God will give Pharaoh the answer he desires" (Genesis 41:16). Joseph proceeds to unfold the divine crop forecast for the next fourteen years. The first seven will be years of blessing and plenty, followed by seven years of famine and shortage. Joseph proposes that with good advance planning, Pharaoh can not only prevent mass starvation but also turn his country into the food supplier for the whole region.

That very day Joseph becomes the second-most powerful man in all of Egypt. Pharaoh installs him immediately with authority to prepare the land for the coming famine.

The court officials are stunned to see this thirty-year-old Hebrew, who has come out of nowhere, being given a royal ring of authority, a gold chain around his neck, a government-issued chariot, and a linen robe. (He finally gets a coat *back*, a very expensive one this time!) Within a matter of hours, people on the street are required to kneel down as his chariot roars past.

The bumper crops begin to come as Joseph predicted, and he is very busy managing the abundance. The whole commodities business of the Middle East looks his way. Senior managers wait outside his office; staff members send him monthly reports. The granaries steadily swell with food for the future.

REVENGE AT LAST?

WHAT WOULD YOU have done with all this power? What would you do if you were Joseph now?

I'll tell you what I might have done. I might have said, "Chariot driver, I have a couple of stops I need to make.

Drive me over to Mrs. Potiphar's house, if you will. I have an old score I need to settle. That woman got me sent to the slammer for a big chunk of my life. It's payback time at last!"

Then I would have headed back to the palace and said to Pharaoh, "Excuse me, but I need to take a week off, if you don't mind. I'm leaving with a couple of army squadrons on a run up to Canaan. I've been waiting to visit my brothers up there for a long, long time." Oooh, how sweet it would have been—vengeance at last!

But not Joseph.

The Bible records that "before the years of famine came, two sons were born to Joseph by Asenath daughter of Potiphera, priest of On. Joseph named his firstborn *Manasseh* and said, 'It is because God has made me *forget* all my trouble and all my father's household'" (Genesis 41:50–51).

> **When Joseph held the first little baby boy in his arms, he said, "I will name this boy Manasseh, because *God has made me forget* all the evil that has been done to me."** ∾

When Joseph held the first little baby boy in his arms, he named him Manasseh, which sounds like the Hebrew word for "forget." Names in those days were not chosen just for their pleasing sound; they always had a meaning.

Joseph could have named his son "Crops" or "Gold" or "Success." He did not. Instead, he focused on the really great thing God had done in his life. As Joseph stood there holding the infant and thinking of all that had happened, he singled out the best of God's blessings as he said, "I will name this boy Manasseh, because *God has made me forget* all the evil that has been done to me."

He didn't say he had learned to forget. He didn't say he had enrolled in a seven-step course or gone to a psychiatrist for help. Instead he said, "God *made me forget.*" God can still touch us supernaturally where no therapist can reach.

Neither was Joseph referring to amnesia. The facts were not erased from his memory. But God took the sting out, so there was no bitterness. The temptation of a mean spirit was conquered. God cleansed Joseph's mind of all the residue that would have naturally festered there from the mistreatment he had suffered. What happiness would his position and wealth have brought if he had been an embittered and angry man?

One of the subtle ways Satan hinders us today is by playing unpleasant tape recordings in our minds over and over and over. People lie in bed at night watching old videos on the inner screen of their hearts. They ride in the car looking out the window but seeing nothing; instead, they daydream about the time someone hurt them, took advantage of them, made them suffer. Hurtful words said by others are heard again and again. Horrible, ugly scenes are repeated hour after hour, day after day, year after year.

> **God can make you forget. He does not obliterate the events, but he can deliver you from the paralysis of the past.** ～

Possibly you are haunted by painful chapters from your past. Some hellish things might have happened to you. Maybe many of them were beyond your control. Whatever the case may be, I want you to know beyond a doubt that God can make you forget. He does not obliterate the events, but he can deliver you from the paralysis of the past.

Earlier I told you about Amalia—but there is more to her story. I remember how, in the early months of her walk with the Lord, I would come onto the platform each Sunday and look up to see her in the same balcony seat. My heart would rejoice as I would notice her with hands raised, praising the Lord and then listening carefully to God's Word.

Every Monday night she was in a home discipleship group. The change in her was dramatic.

Then one Sunday, some months later ... she wasn't there. I was concerned. Silently I prayed, *O God, watch over Amalia!*

The next Sunday, she was back. I saw her in the lobby. "Hi, Pastor Cymbala," she said with a big smile on her face.

"Hello, Amalia. I missed you last Sunday. Is everything okay?"

"Yes, I was away. You know, you preached something about the love of God and forgiveness—so I took the bus upstate to where my father lives."

Her father? I was stunned to hear him even mentioned.

"Yeah—I had to. He lives with his sister up there now, just sitting in a little trailer out in the countryside drinking beer day after day. I forced myself to go see him after all these years."

"How did it go? What did you say?" I asked. It was the last place I expected her to visit.

"I was very nervous. Finally, after the evening meal, I said, 'Pop, I need to talk to you about something. I want you to be serious. You know, I've been remembering the things that happened back when I was a girl. Those years were really hard, and I have to admit that I hated you—'

"'Oh, don't worry about that,' he butted in. 'That was a long time ago; we don't need to talk about that now.'"

Amalia felt the anger well up inside of her again, but she held her composure. She continued, "Yes, we do, Pop. It really hurt me, and I wanted to kill you so many times.... But I came up here this weekend because I want to tell you that I'm a Christian now. I gave my heart to the Lord, and he changed my life.

"You used to be in all of my nightmares. I used to think about you every day. But now, God has made me forget.... Pop, what you did was wrong. But I don't hate you anymore. I forgive you! God can change your life and forgive you, too, Pop. I love you!..."

The man squirmed in his chair at these words from his grown daughter. He quickly found a way to slide off the topic and lighten up the atmosphere. He never did apologize; it proved to be a one-way conversation, which was a great disappointment to Amalia. The rest of the short visit passed without the hoped-for breakthrough or reconciliation.

But Amalia returned home with a peace in her soul for having done what she knew was right. And the seed of God's Word had been planted.

TIME TO FORGET

THE ONLY REASON AMALIA could do what she did is that God is the God of Manasseh, the God who can make us forget.

If you are paralyzed by your past, if Satan is destroying your gifts and your calling by his incessant replaying of old tapes, you're actually being hit by a double whammy. The original damage in the past is one thing—but now you're letting yourself be hurt and sidetracked again by the memory of what happened.

Think of all the people in the church today who go around with an "edge"—some kind of inner anger or constant irritability. Think of others who seem permanently depressed in spirit because something happened, somewhere, sometime. The ugly memories are like chains around them. We should not be ignorant of Satan's devices, and these ugly memories are one of the main weapons in his arsenal.

God wants to remind you today that the same God who has dealt with every sin and wrong deed you've ever done has the ability to make you forget the negative and hurtful things in your life. The grace of God can overcome their power to haunt you.

> **God's people have found that the most precious fruit often grows in the midst of overwhelming difficulties. Faith grows best on cloudy days.** ∿

When a second son came along for Joseph, he chose another significant name. "The second son he named Ephraim and said, 'It is because God has made me *fruitful in the land of my suffering*'" (Genesis 41:52). God taught Joseph that if you put your life in his hands, the worst damage can be turned to good. You can be spiritually fruitful even in the hardest place. In fact, God's people have found that the most precious fruit often grows in the midst of overwhelming difficulties. Faith grows best on cloudy days. Never forget that name of *Ephraim*—"fruitful *in* the land of my suffering."

Every one of us has had painful experiences in life. If you're alive and breathing, somebody sometime has hurt you! In a city such as mine, nasty behavior is everywhere. But you don't have to live in New York City to be hurt. The pain can come from your own family, your in-laws, or other people you genuinely care for.

If you live in that hurt, if those tapes play over and over, you will be paralyzed by them. Every time the Holy Spirit nudges you to step out in faith and do something God wants you to do, this strange bondage to the past will hold you back from God's best for your life.

Do you believe God can set you free, or are you going to keep being a victim of your past? God is the God of Manasseh. He can make you forget. Approach his throne of grace boldly and ask him for that grace to help you right where you need it.

FIVE

~

Can I Trust God
to Lead Me?

It MAY NOT SEEM obvious at first glance, but the way we make decisions in life tells a lot about the kind of faith we have in Jesus Christ. The very process of decision making often reveals our "faith temperature." What does the Bible teach us about this crucial subject?

Some decisions, of course, are about *moral* issues. For example, shall I steal supplies from my employer? We don't need to pray about this one—just read the Bible. There's no need to say, "Lord, is it okay to have this rotten attitude toward my teenager?" The Book already tells us.

Lying is wrong; you don't have to ask God for special insight into the matter. The same thing is true about hating, about prejudice, about marrying a non-Christian. Young women in love will sometimes say to their pastors, "Oh, he's not a believer now, but the Lord showed me he'll come around after the wedding." That cannot be a word from God, for it violates his truth revealed in Scripture. If something is contrary to the Bible, it's wrong. Don't waste your time by praying about it. God gave us a very long "letter" with all kinds of moral instructions. What we need to do is simply read the letter!

Every moral decision, every supposed manifestation of the Spirit, every sermon by a preacher no matter how clever or charismatic—each is to be judged by God's Word. That is what shapes our theology and practice, rather than religious tradition or secular philosophy.

THE FORGOTTEN STANDARD

I AM REPEATEDLY AMAZED as I travel across the country and meet Christians who do not use the Bible as their guide and goal in pursuing spiritual things. Instead, people merely follow the particular spiritual culture into which they were born, never carefully comparing it to the biblical model. In fact, many devote themselves to perpetuating their way of doing things as if they had found it in Scripture itself. Their faith is stale because they are relying on something other than the living God who reveals himself to us through the Bible.

To give an analogy: I was born in a Brooklyn hospital to a Polish mother and a Ukrainian father. I did not ask to have Eastern European parents; I did not ask to be white. That was simply the accident of my birth. To make a big thing about my color or ethnic background is senseless; it just happened to be the way I providentially came into this world. When people get all puffed up about these things, it is really an extension of their own ego. If they had been born a different color or raised in a different country, they would be boasting about that instead.

The same is true about the circumstances of our spiritual birth. The church or denomination where we started out just happened to be where we found ourselves at the time of receiving God's salvation. And as in our natural birth, our initial surroundings gave far-reaching shape to our understanding of things. Our first church atmosphere, with its pastors and teachers, automatically set the definitions for many key words such as *prayer, worship, church, evangelism, God's power, faith*, even *Christian* itself. We didn't first learn those concepts so much from the Scripture as from what we saw around us at church. We unconsciously absorbed a Presbyterian or Baptist or Nazarene or Pentecostal understanding of those important words.

Today those impressions still leap to the forefront of our minds every time we hear the words—whether they are what God intended or not. Thus, instead of coming to the Scriptures like a child, saying, "God, teach me," we go looking for ammunition to back up what we've already embraced. Too often our main goal is to perpetuate the traditions handed down from our elders. We're not really that open to change and growth.

The little church where my parents took me as a boy had some very good qualities to it—but it was also an all-white, mostly Eastern European group in the middle of Bedford-Stuyvesant, one of the best-known black neighborhoods in America! And the church members clearly wanted the church to stay the way it was. They did not seem at all interested in welcoming people who were "different."

> **When we stand before God, we will not be asked, "Were you a good evangelical?" or "Were you a good charismatic?" What will really matter is whether we honestly let God's Word shape our spiritual thinking. ~**

Even though I learned many truths from the Bible there, should I now spend my life trying to replicate that tradition just because it's the place where I started out learning about Jesus? When I stand before God, I will not be asked, "Were you a good evangelical?" or "Were you a good charismatic?" As a matter of fact, God doesn't recognize our divisions. His calling is for us to be Christlike rather than a good member of some man-made denomination.

What will really matter is whether we honestly search God's Word and let it shape our spiritual thinking and values. This is one of the great battles in the Christian life: to approach the Bible without presuppositions, letting it shape us instead of vice versa.

I love what the great John Wesley, catalyst of the Methodist awakening, said in the 1700s: "Would to God that all party names, and unscriptural phrases and forms which have divided the Christian world, were forgot.... I should rejoice ... if the very name [Methodist] might never be mentioned more, but be buried in eternal oblivion."[1] A century later, the equally great Charles Spurgeon, prince of Baptist preachers, said from the pulpit, "I say of the Baptist name, let it perish, but let Christ's name last for ever. I look forward with pleasure to the day when there will not be a Baptist living."[2]

This kind of talk may burst a few bubbles, but here is the truth: Neither your personal background nor mine is the norm! What the Bible teaches is what we should pursue. Whenever any of us encounter something new or different, we should not ask, "Am I used to that when I go to church?" but rather "Do I find this in the Bible?"

WHAT ABOUT THE GRAY AREAS?

SOME DECISIONS IN LIFE are not about moral issues per se, but they simply need *sanctified reasoning*.

For example, the Bible doesn't explicitly say that you should show up for work on time every day. But if you understand God's principles of sowing and reaping, you will be punctual. Also, you are to do your work as if serving the Lord himself.

The Bible doesn't tell you how to respond to your spouse in every situation. But if your husband or wife is upset and discouraged, it's wise for you to be comforting and supportive.

Now, with this foundation, what about the third kind of decision making—those important situations in which we don't have a right-or-wrong element and no Bible passage directly applies? There are many forks in the road where we have to make a choice. What are we to do if we want God's will in everything?

Many people today are making these kinds of decisions without a passing thought of seeking God. They think that as long as they don't lie, kill, steal, or commit adultery, they are in the will of God. They proceed to make other important life decisions based on common sense—or sometimes even less than that. Just "I felt like it!" "My friends are doing it." "My world calls this 'success.'"

When we leave God out of these decisions, we are not really walking in faith. Instead of tapping into God's great resources of wisdom, we rely on mere human ideas.

Isn't it silly to think that the God who gave his own Son for us doesn't also care about the details of our lives?

A faith-filled believer will pray earnestly until he finds God's will for things such as

- Changing jobs
- Dealing with a difficult child
- Choosing a school for your children
- Moving. When you get a job offer in another state, is it just a matter of making more money? Seeing a glossy brochure with lots of green grass? Climbing the ladder of your profession or trade?
- Which believer to marry. (Hint: You're probably not going to find his or her name in the Bible!)

- Buying a home. God has a plan for our lives as detailed as for any person in Scripture. He wants to protect us from being in the wrong place at the wrong time.
- Joining a ministry in the church, such as the choir, the youth ministry, or Christian education.

The all-knowing Creator of the universe *wants* to show us the way in these matters. He has a plan for where we belong and where we don't belong. Therefore we need to seek his direction.

An Inquiring Heart—for God

One of the best Bible examples of a godly person seeking to do God's will is David when he faced a major question at Keilah. The little-known story appears in 1 Samuel 23, during the time David was on the run from King Saul. David had enough trouble of his own trying to protect his modest band of men from the Israelite army—but then word came that this particular town was being threatened by the Philistines.

He began by asking God, "Shall I go and attack these Philistines?" (v. 2). Notice that he didn't assume that just because he had once been anointed by God's prophet, he could win at any time in any place. He knew how important it was to be led by the Lord in every new situation. Not every opportunity for battle meant that he must engage in it.

This is true for us today. Not every Christian cause, not every plea for money—no matter how well intentioned—automatically means that we should respond.

David also knew that if God did lead him into a situation, God's provision would follow. Wherever God leads us, there is an umbrella of protection and supply that stays over our heads. Under that umbrella are the divine resources of wisdom, grace, finance, and all the other things we need to do what God has asked.

That does not mean there won't be problems and difficulties. But wherever the Lord leads, he must then by necessity help us.

However, the umbrella goes only where God leads us to go. If we choose to turn left when God wants us to go right, we cannot expect God to support the plans we made on our own.

Christians today are demonstrating this truth all the time. They are trying to make the umbrella follow them as they make unilateral decisions in life, and it doesn't work. Just because you have declared yourself to be a Christian doesn't mean that God is obligated to supply your needs as you do your own thing.

> **If we choose to turn left when God wants us to go right, we cannot expect God to support the plans we made on our own.** ∾

The Brooklyn Tabernacle Choir has recorded a song based on Psalm 119:133 that says, "Order my steps in Your Word, dear Lord; lead me, guide me every day. . . . / Humbly I ask Thee, teach me Your will; while You are working, help me be still. . . . / Order my steps in Your Word." A minister of music in one church recently told my wife that while the song was a blessing to him personally, his senior pastor had asked him not to use it because "when you have the word of faith, you don't need to ask God to order your steps." In other words, you are so spiritually macho that you can do whatever you choose, and God must go along with you!

This is not in line with the Bible. You cannot tell God what to do and where to go. That is pure spiritual arrogance. How easily we forget that we are not the center of the universe; God is. We must never lose track of the fact that "the world and its desires pass away, but the man *who does the will of God* lives forever" (1 John 2:17).

David was "a man after God's own heart" (see 1 Samuel 13:14; Acts 13:22) because he humbly asked God's direction for his daily life. He knew that if he didn't have the umbrella of God's supply, he had no business tangling with the Philistines outside Keilah. He asked for God's plan, and in this case God said yes—go ahead.

Even then, David came back a second time: "God, my men are not very thrilled about this idea. They say we have enough worries of our own with King Saul chasing us—*so why am I now wanting to take on the Philistines? Should I really do this? Have I truly heard from you?*"

The answer again was yes. "Go down to Keilah, for I am going to give the Philistines into your hand" (1 Samuel 23:4).

This incident reminds us that one of the first rules of spiritual guidance is to assume that we could be wrong. David was humble enough to say to himself, "Possibly I misheard God. I'd better check again." He didn't pretend that he was in constant twenty-four-hour communication with God and above all chance of making a mistake.

One of the first rules of spiritual guidance is to assume that we could be wrong. ~

I remember reading some years ago about a powerful television evangelist who was asked by a reporter from one of the national newsmagazines, "What if you felt God told you to do something, and your whole board of trustees said no?" The preacher quickly boasted, "I'd fire the whole board." It sounded like bold faith, but what he was really saying is that he could never be wrong. Before too long, that man's ministry came crashing down in scandal.

It is not a sign of weakness to look for confirmation. It is often a good idea, in fact, to get a prayer partner, or call a pastor, who can validate your sense of God's will as you inquire of the Lord.

When I first heard about a four-thousand-seat theater in downtown Brooklyn that was for sale and might possibly solve our church's space problems, I got excited. Even though the building was in terrible shape and would require millions of dollars for restoration, I could see the potential for this to become the new Brooklyn Tabernacle.

Very quickly, however, I said to my associate pastors, "You go see it for yourselves and then pray. Unless all six of you feel that God is leading us this way, we won't even present it to the congregation." Would God hide such an important matter from my fellow leaders and reveal it only to me? I don't think so. I also brought other ministers whom I respect, such as David Wilkerson, to see the building. I wanted confirmation that God was leading us this way.

In time, we felt an agreement in our spirits that this step was right. Although the price tag was huge, we moved ahead in faith and confidence.

The story of Keilah shows us that David was firmly convinced in his heart and mind of what he wrote in Psalm 25:9. "He guides the humble in what is right and teaches them his way." In another place, David wrote, "For this God is our God for ever and ever; he will be our guide even to the end" (Psalm 48:14). David triumphed over the Philistines and delivered Keilah, and all of this happened because he inquired of the Lord. David lived by faith, not by sight.

Mᴏʀᴇ Dᴇᴄɪsɪᴏɴs

Bᴜᴛ ᴛʜᴇɴ Kɪɴɢ Sᴀᴜʟ, who was living in the worst kind of spiritual illusion, heard that David was suddenly vulnerable to capture because he had come inside a walled city instead of staying out in rugged terrain. That put a big smile on Saul's face. He was now so deceived in his heart that he even gave the Lord credit for these events! "God has handed him over to me," he said (1 Samuel 23:7).

God had obviously done no such thing. People who are not prayerful and who do not yield to God's will can come to all sorts of wrong conclusions. God was protecting David from Saul, and Saul didn't even have a clue! He immediately called up his army to go capture his nemesis. But David was still inquiring of the Lord. "God, I've heard that Saul is coming, but I'm not sure. Is he really coming?"

Answer: *Yes.*

The next inquiry was "Will these people here in Keilah protect me, since I just saved their necks? Or will they throw me over the wall to Saul?"

Answer: *They'll turn you over.*

So David gathered up his men, and they quickly left town.

Isn't it wonderful that God can even show us who our real friends are and who should not be trusted? He can warn us about what other people are doing behind our backs.

Thus Saul failed to catch David. In other words, success is not by might or power or computers or IQ, but by God's Spirit (Zechariah 4:6). King Saul had better weapons and a far bigger army. But David had the leading of the Holy Spirit. He was in touch with the King of kings.

DOES GOD STILL LEAD?

IN TODAY'S CHURCH, we have a serious shortage of faith in a living, speaking God. Pastors and laity alike do not seem to believe that God really leads and directs. Research by George Barna shows that fewer than 10 percent of churchgoing Christians make important life decisions based on God's Word and seeking his will! In other words, more than 90 percent decide on the basis of their own intelligence, peer opinion, whim, or fancy. They marry people and move to new cities without so much as a ten-minute prayer. Yet every Sunday they sit in church pews singing songs like "Where he leads me, I will follow."

> **Too many church leaders, having been turned off by fanaticism in certain quarters, have stopped believing in an active Holy Spirit at all. The baby has been thrown out with the bathwater.** ∿

Too many church leaders, having been turned off by overblown claims and fanaticism in certain quarters, have stopped believing in an active Holy Spirit at all. The baby has been thrown out with the bathwater. Mention of the Holy Spirit's leading people is scoffed at. If someone says the same thing that Paul said in Acts 16—namely, that the Spirit wanted him to go to one town rather than another—that person is viewed as eccentric. We are strong in presenting our doctrinal positions as correct, but weak in stressing the daily need of being led by God's Spirit.

I want to affirm that God is not dead; he really does communicate today. He's interested in every part of your life, your home, your finances, every kind of decision—and more than just the moral issues. His eye is always on you. He wants to lead you. But you have to believe that he will indeed speak to you when you wait before him in believing prayer, with a yielded heart to do his will.

I fear that unbiblical excesses done supposedly under the inspiration of the Holy Spirit have frightened people off who should really know better. Pastors today operate church services that are so regimented, there is no place for any spontaneous leading of the Holy Spirit. Events are programmed right down to the minute. Song selections are cast in stone for days in advance. There is no allowance for God to lead anyone in another direction—certainly not during the meeting itself. We aim, rather, at being "smooth" and "slick." What we value most are great organization and "having our act together."

As I've said more than once, if God led the Israelites through forty years in the desert, surely he can lead me through a Sunday service. But God has had to teach me over and over about my own need for sensitivity in this matter.

> **If God led the Israelites through forty years in the desert, surely he can lead me through a Sunday service.** ～

Two summers ago in a Sunday afternoon service, our choir was about to sing. As Carol walked past me toward the podium, I asked what songs she had chosen, knowing that she often changes her mind at the last minute as she senses God's direction in a particular meeting. She named two songs. I then took a seat on the front pew in order to better enjoy the choir's ministry.

The first song was about God's great redeeming love, featuring a solo by Calvin Hunt, a young man who has recorded with our choir and now travels in full-time ministry for the Lord. I closed my eyes and let the words sink in.

Somewhere along about the second verse, I sensed the Holy Spirit saying to me, *Go and preach the gospel—right now. Go up and tell them of God's love.*

At first I thought I was maybe just getting a little emotional about an inspirational song. Or maybe Satan was tempting me into some kind of weird behavior.

Then I thought, *My goodness, we haven't even taken the offering yet! This isn't the time to preach and give an invitation; that comes at the end of a meeting, not this early.* (As if God doesn't know what needs to be done in his own church!)

But the impression would not go away. In another thirty seconds I felt that if I did not respond, I would be grieving the Holy Spirit. I silently prayed, *God, I don't want to fail you by not doing your will. I'm going up there at the end of this song. Somehow stop me if I'm wrong.* I felt I had to obey, but I was still nervous about interrupting the meeting.

As the final chord was resolving, I quickly moved up the steps and onto the platform. Carol glanced at me with a quizzical look on her face. I took the microphone from the soloist and said, "Before you go, Calvin, tell the people briefly what God has done in your life."

He went into his story of terrible addiction to crack cocaine and how God had set him free.* Oddly enough, he didn't stumble for words. It was as if he had been prepared for the moment. He gave a powerful statement of the Lord's redemptive power.

---

*For a fuller account of Calvin Hunt's testimony, see chapter 9.

When he finished, I spoke for about ten minutes about the gospel and proceeded to give an invitation. The organist played softly; the choir stayed quietly in place through all this, just waiting to see what would happen next. From all over the auditorium, dozens of people began coming forward to the altar. The sound of weeping could be heard as people were moved upon by the Spirit and now turned to Christ. We prayed with them all, and it was a blessed time of spiritual harvest. Conviction seemed deep and real as the Holy Spirit blessed the simple gospel message.

Eventually I told them to return to their seats, saying, "Well, we haven't taken the offering yet. Let's do that as the choir sings another song." The meeting continued on to its conclusion.

Sometime that following week, the phone rang in our church offices and was answered by Susan, my daughter, who at that time was working in the music department. A man's voice said, "I would like to get the sheet music for such-and-such a song. You sing it in your church, and I want to pass it along to my church here in Texas."

"Well," Susan replied, "I'm very sorry, but we don't have written music for most of the songs we sing. We just do them by memory. Only if we record a song does the publisher then create a written score to sell."

The man was clearly disappointed. "I just heard you all sing it this past Sunday when I was there, and I really want to get that song somehow."

Susan tried to think of something else to say. "Well, I'll mention it to my mother, and maybe she'll decide to put the song on the choir's next album," she said.

There was silence on the line. "Did you say 'your mother'?" the man asked. "Excuse me, but who are you?"

"Susan Pettrey—I'm one of Pastor and Carol Cymbala's married daughters. I work here at the church."

At that, the man began to get a little emotional. "Would you please tell your dad something for me?"

"Yes."

"My family and I were just on a visit to New York for the weekend. We have a nineteen-year-old son who has totally hardened to the things of the Lord. We brought him up to be a Christian, but he has drifted away in the opposite direction. We've been so concerned about him.

"On this trip, we invited him to come with us. I promised him we would take some time to enjoy the city together, but our real plan was to bring him on Sunday to your church in hopes that God would somehow reach him.

"We enjoyed seeing the city all day Saturday. On Sunday, as we took a cab to your church for the afternoon service, I checked our airline tickets once again and realized I'd made a terrible mistake. We wouldn't be able to stay for the whole thing—or else we'd miss our flight home.

"I was kicking myself for not planning better. My son probably wasn't going to hear the message, which was the point of the whole visit.

"But then early in the service—out of nowhere—your dad walked up onto the platform and started to share the gospel. Suddenly my son was standing up with the others and heading for the altar! He just broke down before the Lord, calling out to God for forgiveness. When he came back to the seat, he was a different person.

"We had to leave a few minutes after that for the airport. . . . Just tell your dad that, all the way back to Texas, we could hardly take our eyes off our son in the next seat. This has been the most incredible transformation that you could ever imagine. My wife and I are overjoyed for the great thing God has done."

God changed the whole meeting that afternoon just for the sake of one nineteen-year-old. He knew the need in his life and the timing of flights and knew that something out of the ordinary schedule should occur. God knows things we have no way of knowing. When we don't inquire of the Lord and ask in faith for guidance, we totally miss what he wants to accomplish.

LET GOD GUIDE

WHAT ABOUT THE SITUATIONS you are facing right now? Are there forks in the road that call for a decision to turn one way or the other? Remember that many seemingly unimportant decisions have consequences far beyond what we could ever imagine. Just think how limited we humans are in really knowing the right thing to do. We "see through a glass, darkly" today (1 Corinthians 13:12 KJV), not understanding so many complexities, so many other things hidden from our view. We know nothing of what tomorrow will bring; we're only guessing about the future and what it will hold. Yet these decisions face us again and again.

But our God knows all things and has all power. Even "the king's heart is in the hand of the LORD" (Proverbs 21:1). God knows exactly the plans he has for you, "plans to prosper you and not to harm you, plans to give you a hope and a future" (Jeremiah 29:11). And his desire as a Father is to share these blessed plans with you.

For that to happen will mean yielding to his will for our lives—that's for sure. Then we will be able to hear his voice and sense his direction. It will also mean learning to wait and listen in his presence. But what blessings will be ours as we join the happy company of those who "will neither hunger nor thirst, nor will the desert heat or the sun beat upon them. He who has compassion on them will guide them and lead them beside springs of water" (Isaiah 49:10).

SIX

~

The High Cost
of Cleverness

TRUSTING GOD COMPLETELY to lead and guide us sounds
good in a book such as this, but let's be honest: It can also be
a bit unnerving. Our friends may look sideways at us and
think (or sometimes say) that we are going overboard with all
this "spiritual" stuff. Seeking direction from God goes against
the modern mind's reliance on self. Our culture teaches us to
take charge of our lives and call our own shots.

In sharp contrast to the open, inquiring heart of David,
the Bible tells about another king less than a hundred years
later who had every chance to be as great as David—until he
decided to do what seemed smart and clever to his own mind
instead of what God had said. David, as you will recall, was
followed by his son Solomon, who drifted from God. God
had warned Solomon not to take a large number of wives,
especially foreign women who would draw him away from
the worship of the true God. The mixture with their gods
proved to be fatal, because Solomon ended up building tem-
ples for his wives' gods right in Jerusalem, the place God had
chosen for his presence to dwell.

Near the end of his life, Solomon took notice of a young
man with some leadership ability named Jeroboam and, in
fact, promoted him in the civil service. One day Jeroboam

was innocently walking in a field when a prophet came to him out of the blue, took off his outer garment—and ripped it into twelve pieces! How strange! Giving ten pieces to Jeroboam, the prophet said that God would soon judge Solomon for what he had done and would tear the nation apart—and amazingly, Jeroboam would wind up being king of ten of the twelve tribes. This was followed by some unusual promises from the Lord:

> As for you, I will take you, and you will rule over all that your heart desires; you will be king over Israel. If you do whatever I command you and walk in my ways and do what is right in my eyes by keeping my statutes and commands, as David my servant did, I will be with you. *I will build you a dynasty as enduring as the one I built for David and will give Israel to you* (1 Kings 11:37–38).

Jeroboam must have stood there with his mouth hanging wide open. Why him? He had no claim to anything royal. But out of nowhere, he was selected as God's sovereign choice. Talk about a tremendous "break" at the beginning of your career!

Consider the greatness of these promises to this young man. They are as grand as what the mighty David had received: Control of a nation ... an ongoing dynasty ... the promise of God's abiding presence. Jeroboam, we would say, was set for life.

A STINGING REBUKE

NOW FAST-FORWARD the videotape many years to 1 Kings 14. Jeroboam has indeed risen to the throne of the Northern Kingdom (the ten tribes), just as Ahijah the prophet said that day in the field. But by now, Jeroboam has totally drifted away from God. In this chapter we see the powerful king and his wife with a family crisis: Their little boy has fallen seriously ill, and the worried parents are fearing for his life.

Jeroboam says to his wife, "You know, maybe that old prophet could help. He surely was in touch with God the time he prophesied over me. Why don't you go find him and ask him to pray for our son?"

But Jeroboam knows that his lifestyle has been far from godly. His reputation with Ahijah is at its low point. If his wife shows up to visit, the prophet is likely to scold her or give a bad word of some kind. So he tells her to wear a disguise.

Actually, this wasn't necessary, because by this time, Ahijah is so old that he has gone blind. He can't see whether Mrs. Jeroboam looks like a queen or a scrubwoman. On the other hand, Ahijah is still in close communion with God—and you can't disguise yourself from him. You can act like an Academy Award winner, but God will see through the whole thing in an instant. The minute the woman knocks at the prophet's front door, Ahijah calls out, "Hello, Mrs. Jeroboam-dressed-like-somebody-else—come on in!"

Perhaps she nervously chuckled or tried to make small talk with the old prophet. If she did, it didn't last long. Very quickly the conversation got serious. The woman sat there stunned as Ahijah launched into a shocking prophecy:

> I have been sent to you with bad news. Go, tell Jeroboam that this is what the LORD, the God of Israel, says: "I raised you up from among the people and made you a leader over my people Israel. I tore the kingdom away from the house of David and gave it to you, but you have not been like my servant David, who kept my commands and followed me with all his heart, doing only what was right in my eyes. You have done more evil than all who lived before you. You have made for

yourself other gods, idols made of metal; you have provoked me to anger and thrust me behind your back...."

As for you, go back home. When you set foot in
your city, the boy will die. All Israel will mourn for him
and bury him. He is the only one belonging to Jeroboam who will be buried, because he is the only one
in the house of Jeroboam in whom the LORD, the God
of Israel, has found anything good.

The LORD will raise up for himself a king over
Israel who will cut off the family of Jeroboam. This is
the day! What? Yes, even now. And the LORD will
strike Israel, so that it will be like a reed swaying in the
water. He will uproot Israel from this good land that
he gave to their forefathers and scatter them beyond
the River, because they provoked the LORD to anger
by making Asherah poles. And he will give Israel up
because of the sins Jeroboam has committed and has
caused Israel to commit (1 Kings 14:6–9, 12–16).

What a stinging rebuke! By the time the old man finished, Mrs. Jeroboam must have been sobbing. Within hours
she was going to lose her son, and soon afterward her husband's kingship would be history. In fact, the whole nation
would collapse.

We read this kind of story, and we can't help wondering:
How in the world did this happen! What do you have to do
to go from being chosen by God as the next king ... to the
same prophet now telling you that you're cooked meat—
headed for the garbage pail of history, with no hope of sal-
vaging your kingdom or even your life?

God was saying, *Jeroboam, it's all over. You have provoked
my anger. You are now rejected as king. In fact, I'm going to pun-
ish your whole nation for what you got them to go along with.*

My goodness, what did this man do!

THE PERILS OF GETTING "SMART"

THE ANSWER LIES IN just about eight little verses back in
1 Kings 12, between the first and last meetings with Ahijah.
Jeroboam was king, and one day he got to thinking about his
strategic position. Yes, he was firmly on the throne—but
because of the divided kingdom, God's temple was not in his
territory. It was down south in Jerusalem, the capital of the
Southern Kingdom. Every holy day (two or three times a
year) when his people went to worship, they would have to
go down to his rival's turf. God had made himself clear that
Israelites could not worship and sacrifice their animals just
anywhere and everywhere; they had to go to his one chosen
location in Jerusalem. Hmmm . . .

The Bible says:

> Jeroboam thought to himself, "The kingdom will
> now likely revert to the house of David. If these people
> go up to offer sacrifices at the temple of the LORD in
> Jerusalem, they will again give their allegiance to their
> lord, Rehoboam king of Judah. They will kill me and
> return to King Rehoboam."
>
> After seeking advice, the king made two golden
> calves. He said to the people, "It is too much for you
> to go up to Jerusalem. Here are your gods, O Israel,
> who brought you up out of Egypt." One he set up in
> Bethel, and the other in Dan. And this thing became a
> sin; the people went even as far as Dan to worship the
> one there (1 Kings 12:26–30).

What poignant tragedy lurks in those four words *Jeroboam thought to himself* (v. 26). His whole downfall began
with an attempt at cleverness. He started to strategize.
Instead of simply trusting the promises God had given him,

he tried to "help things out." Otherwise, it seemed, his power would suffer. That's how this tragedy began: Jeroboam thought to himself and forgot about God and his word of promise.

It is horrible when we use human cleverness instead of faith in God. The old gospel song said it well when it advised us just to "trust and obey, for there's no other way to be happy in Jesus."

What Jeroboam ended up doing here was starting his own religion—an insidious mixture of the true and the false. The following verses tell how he "appointed priests from all sorts of people, even though they were not Levites. He instituted a festival on the fifteenth day of the eighth month, like the festival held in Judah" (vv. 31–32). You didn't have to be called by God to be a leader in the Jeroboam religion; you only had to pay money, and you were installed.

God had clearly said in the Second Commandment never to make anything physical as a representation of himself, but Jeroboam now set up two golden calves to anchor the people's devotion. God, in fact, is spirit, and those who want to worship him "must worship in spirit and in truth," as Jesus said (John 4:24). Anything material would never do justice to the greatness of the invisible God, and even if you make something out of pure gold, it can still be wrong to God. He is not impressed with physical appearance or glitter; instead, he looks at the heart. I once heard Anne Graham Lotz say that gold must not mean much to God, for he uses it as paving material in heaven! The saints will walk all over it throughout eternity.

God put this story of Jeroboam in the Bible as a flashing red light to us. It fairly shouts that when unbelief gets into a leader, or anyone else for that matter, it leads to the first bad decision, which leads to the second, which leads to the third, until the momentum builds out of control. God had said to this man out in the field, "If you do whatever I command you and walk in my ways and do what is right in my eyes . . . , I will be with you." But Jeroboam opted to make up his own game plan, and at the end God thundered against him with words so devastating that they make us shudder to read them.

What Jeroboam did—when you think about it—made excellent logic. Any king would want to carefully monitor the movement of his people, right? Trusting God to build the kingdom as he had promised probably seemed too simple. Jeroboam decided to improvise to secure his position of leadership. In fact, unbelief often clothes itself in "being smart." We use cleverness to cover the tracks of our lack of faith. But who can be wiser than God?

....

Unbelief often clothes itself in "being smart." We use cleverness to cover the tracks of our lack of faith. ～

....

As a pastor I sometimes see men in the congregation who are working two or three jobs in order to get ahead financially. They are going to expand their business, make money for a rainy day, or buy a rental property here or a little side business there, and their assets will grow even faster. Yes, it means missing church on Sunday and missing time with their kids, but they use the old saying "Mama didn't raise no fool, you know." In a little while, they tell me, their schedule will lighten up so they can give more attention to the Word and prayer, their service for the Lord, their marriage, their child-raising responsibility . . . soon, but not yet. At the moment, they have to virtually kill themselves for the almighty dollar. These men are sure they can improve on

God's formula: "Seek first [God's] kingdom and his righteousness, and all these things will be given to you as well" (Matthew 6:33).

Jeroboam must have felt *so* smart putting those idolatrous calves in Dan and Bethel—two towns in *his* territory. He told his people he was saving them that long, arduous trip down to Jerusalem. But his new religion was no salvation. It was a dangerous perversion of the true worship of God.

> **In the church today, we are still busy inventing new forms of religion as Jeroboam did. The new models are just as logical and "user-friendly."** ～

In the church today, we are still busy inventing new forms of religion as Jeroboam did. The new models are just as logical and "user-friendly." We must make it *easier on the people*, we say. After all, we need to make church convenient for the busy, modern lifestyle. No one can be expected to sacrifice precious time and energy for the Savior. Subtly, our comfort level becomes the center of the action rather than God. If a weeknight prayer meeting isn't to your particular liking . . . well, hey, God's everywhere, you know! Stay home and do your own thing.

In fact, why even have a prayer meeting? That was only for those old Bible days anyway.

At the heart of "Jeroboam religion" is doing *anything* to keep the crowd. Even as Jeroboam's tragic plan altered God's plan for his people, we have church-growth consultants who know how to slickly play the numbers game. They are experts on what will "work." But sadly, they are blind to the fact that only God "works."

No attendance numbers can hide the fact that our new kind of Christianity is foreign to the Bible and grievous to the Holy Spirit. All over America, churchgoers chafe at a Sunday morning service that runs an hour and ten minutes, but have no problem with three-hour football games on television. Where do we find such a mentality in the New Testament?

I am convinced that in many places today, Jeroboam religion has become so institutionalized that even many in leadership have no clue as to what a true, Spirit-filled church would look like.

TALKING TO OURSELVES

UNBELIEF TALKS TO ITSELF instead of talking to God. How much better it would have been if Jeroboam had analyzed his fears and then taken them to the Lord. If only he had prayed, "O God, I didn't ask to be king, but I know you put me here. The way it looks to me, I could lose everything if my people keep trekking down to Jerusalem. But you said you would be with me and establish my dynasty. So tell me what to do."

Jeroboam didn't do this. Instead he talked to himself.

> **If you are headed in the wrong direction, you can always find a few cronies who will pat you on the back and agree with you.** ~

When we talk to ourselves, we're not talking to anyone very smart, because our outlook is very limited. But if we talk to God, we're talking to someone who knows everything. He knows what he promised in the beginning, and he knows exactly how to fulfill those promises no matter the circumstances.

Jeroboam also turned to some advisers (1 Kings 12:28), who reinforced his disobedience. If you are headed in the wrong direction, you can always find a few cronies who will pat you on the back and agree with you. What Jeroboam needed was a godly prayer partner who would have stopped him cold by saying, "Wait a minute—didn't God give you a promise in the beginning? How can doing wrong bring about something good?"

This is not a story about embezzlement, or meeting a woman in a motel, or smoking some illegal drug. This is a story about simply drifting away from God and his Word. *Yes, I'm aware of what God said—but in the present situation, I really feel the need to do such-and-such.* Instead of focusing on the faithfulness of God, we focus on what the circumstances seem to dictate.

But faith enables us to see God on top of all our problems. If we see only the problems, we get depressed and start making wrong decisions. When we have faith, we see God bigger than any mountain, and we know he is going to take care of us.

> **When you're walking in unbelief, you get out of bed saying, "Oh, no! Is this the day I'm going to lose it all?" The glass is always half-empty.** ∼

If *God* is for you, it doesn't matter how many demons in hell try to oppose you. If *God* is for you, it doesn't matter what your opponents whisper in the ears of people. Unbelief has a devious way of envisioning negative things. When you're walking in faith, you get out of bed in the morning saying, "Surely goodness and love will follow me all the days of my life, and I will dwell in the house of the LORD forever" (Psalm 23:6). But when you're walking in unbelief, you get out of bed saying, "Oh, no! Is this the day I'm going to lose it all?" The glass is always half-empty.

Those who walk in faith are still realists. They often admit that they don't know how everything is going to work out; but they insist that their God will supply nonetheless.

LISTENING TO THE VOICE OF FAITH

JEROBOAM'S WORRIES EVENTUALLY led to fatalism. Over time he went from imagining the loss of the people's loyalty all the way to fear that "they will kill me" (1 Kings 12:27)! Unbelief loves to paint the bleakest picture it can. It loves to get us mumbling to ourselves, *I'm not going to make it. I just know this is going to turn out terrible. The future is bound to crash on me.*

Let me tell you that God, who began a good work in you, is not about to stop now. After sending his Son to die for your sins, after saving you at such incredible cost, why would he let you fail now?

Let us declare war this very moment on the cleverness that is really a mask for unbelief. Bring your problem to God, as a little child would, in total confidence that he alone can fix whatever is broken. Open your Bible and let the Holy Spirit plant in you the seeds of a fresh faith that will blossom as you wait on the Lord. Don't give up asking, seeking, and knocking—no matter what pressure you feel to "do something."

How can our heavenly Father do anything but respond to our persistent prayer of faith? Jesus said, "Will not God bring about justice for his chosen ones, who cry out to him day and night? Will he keep putting them off? I tell you, he will see that they get justice, and quickly. However, when the Son of Man comes, will he find faith on the earth?" (Luke 18:7–8).

SEVEN

∾

Faith Runs on
a Different Clock

REMEMBER THE FATHER from Texas who brought his wayward son to church and was worried about catching a flight?
He got an eye-opening lesson that God's timetable is not
always the same as ours. The man thought his prayers had
gone for naught because of an airline schedule, while God
had everything under control to achieve his purposes regardless of how things seemed to be unfolding.

Many of our struggles with faith have to do with timing.
We believe, at least in theory, that God will keep his promises—
but when? If the answer does not come as soon as we expect,
fear begins to assault us, and then soon we are tempted to
"throw away [our] confidence," ignoring the fact that "it will
be richly rewarded" (Hebrews 10:35). How many times have
you prayed for a son's or daughter's salvation? Are you still
praying? Do you really believe God is listening?

It would be a good idea if we all just admitted that we
need to learn about God's way of doing things. One of the
best illustrations of divine pacing in the Bible is the story of
Zechariah and Elizabeth, which is laid out in elaborate detail.
In fact, the Gospel of Luke has almost as much to say about
these two senior citizens as it has about Mary and Joseph.
Why didn't Luke write as Mark did in his Gospel and just cut

to the chase: "God sent a forerunner, John the Baptist, to tell people to repent and get ready for the great Messiah"—and that would have been enough?

> **Many of our struggles about faith have to do with timing. We believe, at least in theory, that God will keep his promises—but when?** ~

No, God wanted to teach some special lessons through the details of this story.

Zechariah was an elderly priest who had no children. Folks in town naturally assumed he and his wife would never have a family. Not only was Elizabeth barren, but she was now too old to give birth.

Zechariah was simply going about his work in the temple one day when an angel appeared and startled him with a message from God. "Do not be afraid, Zechariah; your prayer has been heard. Your wife Elizabeth will bear you a son, and you are to give him the name John. He will be a joy and delight to you, and many will rejoice because of his birth" (Luke 1:13–14). The boy, in fact, would turn out to be John the Baptist.

GOD MAKES SOME VERY ODD CHOICES

RIGHT AWAY THIS STORY shows us that God's way of doing things is very different from ours. Even the way he chooses to order events holds specific lessons for us.

If you were God in heaven looking down on the earth, and you could choose any set of parents across the land of Israel to raise this important messenger, whom would you pick? No doubt you or I would select a healthy young woman about twenty-three or twenty-four years old, at the height of her childbearing years, with plenty of energy to get up in the middle of the night with this baby and do all the things a mother must do. We would look for a husband perhaps twenty-four or twenty-five, physically strong, and well established in his career. We would also want this couple to have money and a good education, so the child would have a stimulating environment. They should live in a safe neighborhood in an upscale suburb, with the best schools and all kinds of cultural enrichment nearby.

The couple should also be planning on having one or maybe two more children after this first one, so the boy would not grow up alone. After all, peer companionship is important. Remember, this baby has a divine mission in life.

But what does God do? He casts his eye all across the land of Israel and finds a woman who can't have a baby! While all her friends in the little desert town seem to have gotten pregnant, she has remained childless. Then God waits and waits until she is past childbearing years, so that even if she *could* have conceived a child, it is now too late. She is doubly disqualified as a special mother for this special child.

And the God of heaven says, "That's the one! As the boy grows up, from the time he is nursed to the time he grows into manhood, his mother will be able to tell him over and over the story of his birth, the miracle of his aged parents— all of it reinforcing in his tender mind that 'nothing is impossible with God' (Luke 1:37)."

Many times in life, God waits while a situation goes from bad to worse. He appears to let it slip over the edge, so that you and I say, "There's *no way* now for this ever to work out." But that is the point when the omnipotent God intervenes in our hopelessness and says, "Oh, really? Watch this...!"

More than worrying about John the Baptist's schooling or music lessons or anything else, God wanted him to grow up in a godly atmosphere of praise and worship. At least once a day that old, devoted couple must have looked at that little boy and said, or at least thought, "Our God is an awesome God! Blessed be his name!"

So many times when we get into emergencies and the situation seems totally hopeless—it's actually a setup. God wants to do something great. He wants to demonstrate his power, so that his name will be praised in a new and greater way. The next generation will hear all about it. After all, their spiritual nurture is far more important than mere material things. Did you know that parents can feed their children three nutritious meals a day and put the latest $120 sneakers on their feet—and still deprive them spiritually? To withhold from children the knowledge of the wonderful and loving God who created them is the worst kind of parenting. They cannot truly live without Jesus, regardless of the top-drawer education they might receive.

> **So many times when we get into emergencies and the situation seems totally hopeless— it's actually a set-up. God wants to do something great.** ~

Even beyond our own families, God wants to publish everywhere through our lives the testimony of his mighty power and salvation. Beyond our head knowledge of Bible verses, he wants to demonstrate tangibly that he has never changed. Let's not forget the next time we face the "impossible" that our God is *still* an awesome God.

GOD IS DRAWN TO PRAYER

NOTICE ALSO HOW MUCH of this story is centered around prayer and worship.

Zechariah, the old priest, trudged from his home to Jerusalem to serve his rotation in the temple. His assignment that day, Luke 1:9 says, was to "burn incense"—an act of worship. The placing of spices on the fire on the altar resulted in a sweet scent arising to God. Meanwhile, at that specific hour in the temple courtyard, a large crowd of people "were praying outside" (Luke 1:10). They were all opening their hearts to God as best they knew, reaching out and communing with him—the highest activity that any human being can aspire to.

That was the moment when the angel appeared.

God could have shown up at any time, but over and over in the Bible, he revealed himself when people began to pray.

- Peter went up on a rooftop to pray (Acts 10). There God gave him a vision about reaching out to other ethnic groups with the gospel.
- The early church gathered after some persecution to pray. Suddenly, "the place where they were meeting was shaken. And they were all filled with the Holy Spirit" (Acts 4:31).
- The twelve disciples never asked Jesus to teach them to preach. But they did say, "Lord, teach us to pray" (Luke 11:1). They saw something about his communion with the Father that was so outstanding that they couldn't help saying, "Help us to pray like *that*."

The minute the angel showed up, Zechariah panicked. The first words out of the angel's mouth were "Do not be afraid, Zechariah; your prayer has been heard" (Luke 1:13).

What prayer? Obviously, his many prayers over the years for Elizabeth to have a child.

By this stage in life, Zechariah had probably stopped thinking that fatherhood was even possible for him. *But it didn't matter;* his many years of praying in faith were still on record! When prayer comes from a sincere heart, it rises into God's presence *and stays there.* The more prayers you add, the more they collect in heaven. They don't evaporate like a gas. They remain before God. Remember how another angel said to Cornelius, the Roman centurion, "Your prayers and gifts to the poor have come up as a memorial offering before God" (Acts 10:4). Those prayers didn't just float away. They added up, until the day when God sent a special messenger to this man.

When we seek God for answers, we must persevere in prayer, letting it build up day after day until the force of it becomes a mighty tide pushing over all obstacles. No wonder God says his house is supposed to be known as a house of prayer—not merely a house of preaching or of singing, but especially of prayer. How else will we receive great answers from God unless we persevere in prayer?

> **How must God feel every Sunday when, all over the nation, so many people gather in churches but do so little actual praying?** ∽

How must God feel every Sunday when, all over the nation, so many people gather in churches but do so little actual praying? Congregations make time in the weekly schedule for everything from basketball leagues to weight-loss classes, but they can't seem to find a slot for a prayer meeting. The Lord waits to bless his people with his abundant supply, but we don't take the time to open the channel. What a terrible epitaph: "You do not have, because you do not ask God" (James 4:2).

God is drawn to prayer. He delights in communion with us. Prayer releases his blessing into our lives.

GOD DOES NOT APPRECIATE SECOND-GUESSING

WHEN ZECHARIAH RAISES his objection (Luke 1:18), he betrays the fact that he apparently hasn't been praying for a child recently. In his mind, he pictures Elizabeth back home in the small town. She is certainly no spring chicken.

His question—"How can I be sure of this?"—is logical, I suppose. You might think that Gabriel would reply, "Well, old man, let me tell you: God is going to help you. He will empower you and your wife, and everything will work out fine."

No. The angel has already declared, on God's behalf, what is going to happen—so there's nothing left to discuss. Facts have been stated: Elizabeth *will* have a son, you must give him the name John, he will be great in the sight of the Lord, etc., etc. Case closed.

But Zechariah questions God's ability—and suddenly there is a strong reaction. The angel announces that the old man will lose his speech for nine months! If Gabriel had been from Brooklyn, he might have said, "Yo! What's your problem? I'm Gabriel, the angel God sent to tell you this good news. If you don't want to believe it, then you won't speak at all till you see the baby!"

When God sends his divine promise, he is very grieved and saddened if his people do not believe him. It breaks his father-heart to hear his own children say, "Well, maybe ... I hope so ... but how could that be, really, now? ... Yes, God has said he will bring back my daughter—but, you know, she's so hard...."

Is it not enough that God declared he would do something? He doesn't have to explain any of his methods in advance. "Nothing is impossible," remember?

> **God gets fairly irritated—and rightly so—with Christians who refuse to believe, who question his veracity, who start backpedaling after he has said he's going to do something.** ~

Zechariah's mouth is zipped shut. This response gives potent meaning to the oft-quoted words of Hebrews 11:6: "Without faith it is impossible to please God." God gets fairly irritated—and rightly so—with Christians who refuse to believe, who question his veracity, who start backpedaling after he has said he's going to do something. The Lord wants to shout, "Will you please just *trust me!* Is anything too hard for God?"

One time Jesus said to a woman whose brother had died and who thought it was therefore too late for Jesus to help, "Did I not tell you that if you believed, you would see the glory of God?" (John 11:40). Jesus then proceeded to the cemetery and called Lazarus right up out of his grave.

The great battle of our spiritual lives is "Will you believe?" It is *not* "Will you try harder?" or "Can you make yourself worthy?" It is squarely a matter of believing that God will do what only he can do. That is what God honors. He treasures those who respond and open their hearts to him. He's looking for faith so strong that it will anchor on his

Word and wait for him, the One who makes everything beautiful in its time.

INNOCENCE AT RISK

I SHALL NEVER FORGET the Sunday night we finally persuaded shy, soft-spoken Wendy Alvear to stand in front of our congregation and tell fifteen hundred people her story. She started off hesitantly, telling about her growing-up years in Williamsburg, the Brooklyn neighborhood right at the east end of the Williamsburg Bridge that comes across from lower Manhattan. The people on those streets were a curious but harmonious mixture of Hasidic Jews and Puerto Rican immigrants like her parents. Even the drug addicts, she remembers, were nice to the children on the sidewalk.

> The great battle of our spiritual lives is "Will you believe?" It is *not* "Will you try harder?" or "Can you make yourself worthy?" ∼

Growing up the second of four children in the family, Wendy characterized herself as "a romantic," dreaming of the day she would get married to a handsome husband and raise a houseful of children of her own. She loved kids and was an enthusiastic baby-sitter. Her sunny disposition was only partly suppressed by the strict-minded Spanish church she attended with her mother and siblings three or four nights a week. There she learned about Jesus and soon welcomed him into her life—even though they said he had a long list of rules that she had to obey. Wendy's father was not a Christian, but he didn't seem to mind the rest of his family going to church.

One of the rules in that church was that women and girls always wore skirts. When Wendy's ninth-grade class at school went on a field trip to an amusement park, she felt uneasy. A friend said, "I'll bring some pants from home for you to borrow, okay?" And Wendy gladly took her up on it.

"The only trouble was, the trip ran late," Wendy recalls, "and we didn't get back to school at the appointed time. When we finally arrived, my mother was there waiting to pick me up. I was trapped! I could do nothing but get off the bus and face the music."

That was the point when the attractive young adolescent asked to stop going to church. Her father, of course, supported her request. While alone in her room, however, she did feel the need to offer an apology to God: "I'm sorry about this— but I'll go back to church when I get married. I promise."

By her senior year, Wendy's life was taken up with dance clubs, smoking, and drinking—but "no hard drugs," she affirmed to God. Her first real boyfriend, who went by the Hispanic nickname of Papo, was battling to overcome heroin. "I thought I could help him," she admits with a slight smile. "I would plead with him not to do drugs. So as a compromise, we'd drink wine together instead." Papo may have in fact consumed less heroin as a result, but his dark-haired girlfriend became a steady drinker.

One night in McCarren Park, the two of them and a large group of friends were hanging out after midnight, the boys playing basketball and the girls just talking nearby. All had had plenty to drink. Wendy relaxed on a park bench and, in time, fell asleep, while the others gradually drifted away, leaving her alone.

She awoke with a start when she felt the rough hands of a man moving over her body. Her eyes flew open. Papo and the group were nowhere to be seen—just this stranger, intent on having his way with her.

"In my panic, I tried to think what to do. Suddenly an idea came to me. I said to him, 'Okay, okay—this is cool! But you know what? I have to use the ladies room first. . . . I live just a couple of blocks away. Let's go there!'"

Amazingly, the gullible fellow agreed. In fact, the distance was more like fifteen blocks! "Here he was, walking me all the way to my building, where I cheerfully said, 'I'll run upstairs and be right back!' Thank God, he wasn't too swift." Once in her parents' apartment behind locked doors, of course, Wendy promptly went to bed.

The next morning, she soberly said to herself, "Wow!— I was really in danger last night, wasn't I? How come Papo left me there on the park bench, anyway?" The process of finding a nice young man to marry was turning out to be harder than it looked.

MR. RIGHT AT LAST?

THE NEXT BOYFRIEND was better, at least in some ways: He was drug-free and had a job as a shoe salesman. His name was John. Wendy had known him from the beginning of high school, and her family found him to be respectful and polite. There was the complication that he, being four or five years older than Wendy, had already been through a short and turbulent marriage, resulting in a daughter for whom he was now responsible. But the future looked promising.

"I was overjoyed," says Wendy. "Here was the man of my dreams. I had a solid job with New York Life Insurance Company, and he was doing well, too. When we got engaged on Valentine's Day, it was the highlight of my life."

They began planning for a summer wedding. But then, for some inexplicable reason, John's mood began to change. He became less gracious toward Wendy, and then abrupt and demanding. Were the bad memories of his past marriage starting to stir the waters? Wendy couldn't tell. He wanted physical intimacy, and when she declined until the wedding, he grew upset.

Within three months Wendy learned that John was seeking favors elsewhere. She promptly broke the engagement.

"Now I was really lonely," she says. "And I wasn't close enough to God to ask for his help. I sank into more drinking. And it seemed that whenever I would drink, I would become angry and aggressive—which caused me to ruin some parties and alienate my friends. I gradually withdrew into depression, just coming home from work each day and hiding in my room until the next morning."

This unhappy lifestyle continued until Wendy was twenty-five. Her father became suddenly ill and passed away. Shortly before, he had become a Christian, and the two of them had enjoyed some warm conversations. His death was a heavy blow to Wendy.

Two weeks after her father's burial, Wendy was finally ready to listen to the Lord. *Wendy, it's time to come home,* he seemed to say to her—and she responded. A great relief swept over her spirit as the heavenly Father she had long spurned welcomed her back into his arms.

By the next Sunday she was at the Brooklyn Tabernacle. The old legalism was missing—she even saw some women there in pants!—but instead, the love and grace of God pervaded the atmosphere. Wendy started to grow in the Lord, build Christian friendships, join the singles group, and sing in the choir.

Years went by. Wendy was a blessing to us all. Inside, of course, her desire to be married was as strong as ever. She was saying to herself, *Okay, God—where is he?* And God seemed not to give an answer to that heartfelt question. Meanwhile, she watched one friend after another get married in the church.

Wendy's thirtieth birthday came and went . . . then her thirty-fifth. By now she was worrying that maybe God's plan for her life did not include marriage or motherhood. That possibility saddened her greatly. We didn't see quite as many smiles on her face.

One Saturday, alone in her home, she set aside a time to seek the Lord. A couple of her sisters were going through deep waters, and she wanted to intercede for them. But even more, she wanted to talk to God about her singleness. She began to complain. The prayer time "turned into a full-blown pity party," she admits.

In response, the Lord seemed to say to her, "Wendy, you are hurting because you've taken your eyes off of me and put them on the situation. You have forgotten that I am the source of all happiness. Circumstances don't matter. Keep your eyes on me."

A dark cloud lifted as she said in response, "All right, Lord—I will place my desire for a husband 'on the altar,' so to speak. I will give it to you. Go ahead and burn it up like a sacrifice. Consume it! I will stop whining about this."

Peace came back into her soul, and Wendy went on with her life. The only change was that, after seventeen years at New York Life, she quit that job and accepted an invitation to join the Brooklyn Tabernacle staff. What an even greater blessing she became.

Surely Not . . .

About a year later, a man came seeking help from Pastor Michael Durso at Christ Tabernacle, Queens, one of our daughter churches. During an appointment in the pastor's office, he gave his life to Christ. His name was John Alvear—the same John who had been in Wendy's life years before.

Soon John showed up at the Brooklyn Tabernacle, looking for Wendy. A couple of choir members passed the word along to her, which triggered sudden apprehension. She thought, "John wants to come back into my life? Oh, no! I can't handle this. It must be a snare from the Enemy!' People told me he had gotten saved and was serving the Lord now, but still—"

Wendy avoided John for a good while, only agreeing at last to go out with him as part of a large group of friends. John's attitude had indeed changed; he had become a new creation in Christ. He and Wendy began dating, and a warm affection blossomed.

Wendy was still concerned about getting involved with "a babe in Christ," as she puts it. After all, she had now been walking with the Lord as an adult for more than a decade, and John was only four months old in his Christian life. She urged him to talk to Pastor Dan Iampaglia, one of the Brooklyn Tabernacle associates at the time.

John and Dan had lunch together. The next day in the office, Wendy wanted to know how it had gone.

"He seems very nice, very sincere," said Pastor Iampaglia. "I believe his walk with the Lord is genuine."

Even that was not enough. Next, Wendy wanted to talk to me. I told her, "Don't be afraid of what God is doing in your life. John is a very special man."

Wendy still worried about whether she could really be finding God's choice for her life after all this time. Then one day, John called her at work. They began to talk about their relationship. With utmost sincerity, John said, "I am just trying to follow God's plan for me—that's the most important thing in my life. In fact, I never stopped loving you. But I want God's will so badly—even if it doesn't include you." At that, his voice broke as the tears came. Wendy began to cry as well.

And that is how, at the age of thirty-seven, Wendy finally became a bride. Their wedding was an explosion of joy. What a special couple they became in the life of our church!

Wendy feared that she had waited too long to ever become a mother. But by the next year, little Jeniece Rebecca was welcomed into their home. Then, at the age of thiry-nine, Wendy gave birth to John Eric. They were recently able to purchase their own home in the borough of Staten Island, across the harbor from Brooklyn.

As Wendy closed her remarks to the church that night, she said, "Whatever you do, keep seeking God's will for your life. He will do it! Don't settle for anything less. Wait for God—he knows how to give you the best."

LET GOD DO IT HIMSELF

THE HARDEST PART of faith is often simply to wait. And the trouble is, if we don't, then we start to fix the problem ourselves—and that makes it worse. We complicate the situation to the point where it takes God much longer to fix it than if we had quietly waited for his working in the first place.

The timing of God is often a mystery to us, and even sometimes a frustration. But we must not give up. We must not try to arrange our own solutions. Instead, we must keep on believing and waiting for God. We will not be alone as we patiently wait for his answer in his time. We will be joining the great host of saints down through the ages whose faith was tested and purified by waiting for God.

This is what David meant when he testified, "I waited patiently for the LORD" (Psalm 40:1). Instead of taking matters into his own hands, or despairing of God's help at all, David learned to wait for God to work out his plan in his time. But after a while, God proved faithful as always, for David continued his story by adding, "He turned to me and heard my cry. He lifted me out of the slimy pit, out of the mud and mire; he set my feet on a rock and gave me a firm place to stand" (vv. 1–2). What happened was all-glorious, but it came only after a time of waiting in faith.

> **The timing of God is often a mystery to us, and even sometimes a frustration. But we must not give up. We must not try to arrange our own solutions. ～**

Don't give up today, and don't give in to the voices of unbelief and impatience. Remember these words from a beautiful song I have enjoyed so much over the years:

Keep believing in what you know is true;
Keep believing—you know the Lord will
  see you through.
When troubles rise in your life, and you don't
  know what to do,
You'll be fine if you just keep believing.[1]

EIGHT

~

Overcoming
Discouragement

W HEN SOMEONE SAYS something outlandish here in New York City, one of the common put-downs is "Get real!" or "Be real!"—in other words, please return to Planet Earth with the rest of us and talk some sense. No matter where you live, I'm sure you've heard the same kind of criticism—that someone is being "unrealistic." That person is not like the rest of us intelligent folks who live happily with both feet firmly planted in the real world.

Let me tell you about a time when a group of very smart folks showed great *realism* based on obvious facts—and the results were disastrous. Moses had brought the Hebrew people out of Egypt in response to God's promise that he would give them a wonderful land. After receiving the Ten Commandments and other instructions from God, Moses sent twelve spies to check out the real estate of Canaan. God had already said he would give it to the Hebrews; in fact, he had begun making that promise several hundred years before, to Abraham.

Moses sent the twelve simply to gather information, not to form opinions. All he assigned them to do was to "see what the land is like and whether the people who live there are strong or weak, few or many. What kind of land do they live in? Is it good or bad? What kind of towns do they live in? Are they unwalled or fortified? How is the soil? Is it fertile or poor? Are there trees on it or not?" (Numbers 13:18–20). Sounds like a fifth-grade geography teacher giving her class a research assignment in the encyclopedia.

Nobody asked the spies to draw conclusions. Nobody asked them to gauge the prospects for military success. God had already guaranteed that.

When they returned from their field trip, however, ten of the spies went far beyond their assignment. They reported the data accurately—and then immediately got "realistic" by adding, "We can't attack those people; they are stronger than we are. . . . The land we explored devours those living in it. All the people we saw there are of great size. . . . We seemed like grasshoppers in our own eyes, and we looked the same to them" (vv. 31–33). This report went against all God had promised, and thus their common-sense realism affected the destiny of a whole generation of Israelites. The people began to panic and murmur against God.

Who could have predicted that these men would cause a historic turning point? Who could have known that this report and the discouragement it triggered would provoke God to the point of saying, "All right—that's it! You will *not* go into Canaan now after all; you will spend another thirty-eight years wandering in this desert instead. In fact, nearly all of you here today will never get to the Promised Land at all. You're going to grow old and die out here on these sands."

What is so amazing is that these people had already seen God do many supernatural things. They had seen the ten remarkable plagues of Egypt. They had walked out into the Red Sea by faith, believing that the miraculous restraint on the water would hold firm until they got across. They had seen God shake a mountain with thunderous force. They had watched Moses bring down the divine law, written by the finger of God on a stone.

But now they chose to believe a human report rather than God's promise. The Bible calls the ten spies' summary "a bad report" (Numbers 13:32). The King James Version is even stronger: "an evil report." What was so wicked about it? After all, its facts were accurate. The Israelites were realistically no match for the fierce tribes of Canaan. But this report of the spies was full of unbelief and spawned deep discouragement among God's people. God was provoked by their distrust.

> **Do we believe what our feelings and circumstances tell us, or do we believe what God has promised to do?** ∾

Thousands of years later, little has changed for God's people: Do we believe what our feelings and circumstances tell us, or do we believe what God has promised to do?

CONQUERING "THE BIG D"

THIS STORY TEACHES us several things:

It's not starting the race that counts; it's finishing. These people, by giving in to discouragement, never saw the fulfillment of God's promise in their lives. Today we sometimes fool ourselves with a theology that mumbles, "Well, God will take care of everything somehow. It doesn't matter what we do; the Lord is sovereign, you know." Not exactly!

The truth is that without faith, it is impossible to please God. We receive things—even the things God has promised us—only if we have faith. As Jesus said to two blind men, "According to your faith will it be done to you" (Matthew

9:29). This means that my life or yours has only as much of God as our faith permits. The promises of God are appropriated only by faith. God is looking for a people who will believe him and take him at his word no matter what the circumstances say or what other people are telling us.

Joshua and Caleb, the "minority" spies, were two such people who took God at his word. "We should go up and take possession of the land," they said, "for we can certainly do it" (Numbers 13:30). Yet they had seen the same enemies the other spies had seen. This is why God gave that wonderful compliment in Numbers 14:24, saying, "My servant Caleb has a different spirit and follows me wholeheartedly." As a result of this willingness to side with God's promise, Caleb and Joshua got to enter the land. The other ten spies, however—and a million or two other people—died along the way.

Pressures are exerted all through life to make us want to lie down and quit. The most spiritual person in the world is tempted to get discouraged. I remember seeing a television interview with Billy Graham and his delightfully honest wife, Ruth. The host, David Frost, said something like, "So you two pray together and read the Bible together on a regular basis. But tell me the truth, Mrs. Graham: In all these years of living with Billy, have you never had problems or disagreements? Have you never even once contemplated divorce?"

"Not once," she fired back. "Murder, a few times—but not divorce!"

Obviously, there are challenges to overcome even in the Billy Graham home. You and I have our share of difficulties, but the most important thing is to finish our lives still trusting God, as the evangelist and his wife are doing.

In fact, the greatest battle on earth has not been fought on the Normandy beaches or on Iwo Jima or in the Persian Gulf. Rather, it has raged inside your heart and mine: the battle to believe. The just not only must begin by faith but continue to live by it as well (Romans 1:17). Faith is as essential to everyday living as it is to initial salvation.

As Athanasius, the early church father, said, "I can do nothing without the help of God, and that from moment to moment; for when, so long as we are on the earth, is there a single instant in which we can say we are safe from temptation or secure from sin?"[1] Only God's grace can keep us, and that grace is activated by faith.

Caleb walked in this attitude of faith his whole life. The book of Joshua shows him as an old man, long after the spying trip, making a rousing speech to his equally elderly partner Joshua, who is now in charge of the nation:

> I was forty years old when Moses the servant of the LORD sent me from Kadesh Barnea to explore the land. And I brought him back a report according to my convictions, but my brothers who went up with me made the hearts of the people melt with fear. I, however, followed the LORD my God wholeheartedly....
>
> Now then, just as the Lord promised, he has kept me alive for forty-five years since the time he said this to Moses, while Israel moved about in the desert. So here I am today, eighty-five years old! I am still as strong today as the day Moses sent me out; I'm just as vigorous to go out to battle now as I was then. Now give me this hill country that the LORD promised me that day. You yourself heard then that the Anakites were there and their cities were large and fortified, but, the LORD helping me, I will drive them out just as he said (Joshua 14:7–8, 10–12).

Caleb never retired! He just kept going, and faith kept him young and strong in heart. To the end, he wanted to fight the Lord's enemies no matter how entrenched they seemed. He knew that God could do anything, and he wanted to be a part of God's action as long as he could. Discouragement never seemed to sap his spiritual vigor.

Now we see the importance of the verse in Hebrews that says, "Let us not give up meeting together, as some are in the habit of doing, but let us *encourage one another*—and all the more as you see the Day approaching" (10:25). Going to church and having Christian fellowship should never leave us discouraged—there's enough of that everywhere around us. Even if God searches our hearts very directly concerning sin, we should still leave the building encouraged, because once the Spirit reveals our disobedience, he will bring cleansing and strength to our hearts. He will cause us to see his promises and his love in a new, clear light.

One of the primary names for the Holy Spirit is "the Comforter." And one of the primary names for the devil, who likes to impersonate the Holy Spirit, is "the Accuser." The Comforter encourages us and builds us up. The Accuser is in the business of tearing us down.

> **One of the primary names for the Holy Spirit is "the Comforter." And one of the primary names for the devil, who likes to impersonate the Holy Spirit, is "the Accuser."** ～

Wives who are negative and discouraging can sometimes cause more damage in their homes than any drug addiction. Husbands who talk down to their families and go against the promises of God are walking on dangerous ground. They are following in the footsteps of the ten spies! They are once again repeating, "Yes, but . . ." and "It sounds good, but we can't. . . ."

Americans are waging a mighty war against "the Big C"—cancer. The people and the government are investing huge sums to fight this horrible disease that invades millions of people. If only in the spiritual realm we would give equal effort to strike down "the Big D"—discouragement. It kills not the body, but the soul. Its dreadful toll on the people of God is greater than anyone could calculate.

> **The only hospital that can treat "the Big D"—discouragement—is the hospital of the Word of God, which is managed by the Holy Spirit.** $\sim$

I have often sat in my office, trying to counsel couples who know that they are in trouble. They are entirely accurate as to the surface facts of their situation. But they are also so negative and pessimistic that you want to scream. There is no faith or expectancy for what God has promised to do for his people.

Try to count all the times in the Bible that God says to us, "Be encouraged," or "Fear not," or "Be not afraid." The battle is always not about giving in to what we see around us, but about holding onto God's promises.

The only hospital that can treat "the Big D" is the hospital of the Word of God, which is managed by the Holy Spirit. Only there can our spirits be lifted.

LOOSE TALK

THE ENEMY USES ordinary people to discourage us. Who caused all the trouble that day in the desert? Not some demon with a pitchfork. Just people talking. People who were part of the

Israelite community, not pagan strangers. People everyone knew and even respected. People chosen by Moses himself.

It is very important for us to watch whom we talk to. Some voices are *not* good for us. Some folks need to be avoided. Those who are negative and don't really believe God will have an effect on your spirit. God has to give you wisdom on how to change the subject or even extract yourself from the situation without offending.

LOOSE EMOTIONS

DISCOURAGEMENT IS AT the heart of other reactions. Numbers 14:1 says, "That night all the people of the community raised their voices and wept aloud." The camp broke down into one massive pity party. While tears before God are usually valued highly in the pages of Scripture, this was a crying produced by unbelief and fear.

I have heard certain people pray with emotion, but their lack of faith made it sound more like the Israelites that day in their tents. They were not really pouring out their souls to God in faith, but rather venting their fear and frustration.

> **Let's stop blaming our unbelief on the pastor we once had, on our childhood, on circumstances, or on anything else. There is no excuse for not believing in the Lord.** ～

The Israelites' tears soon led to blasphemy. They accused God of bringing them out of Egypt only to die! (v. 3). Think of the blasphemy of that—and yet it all started with simply doubting whether the Lord would do what he promised. Now they had sunk to saying terrible things about the God of Israel.

Then (v. 4) they talked about getting rid of Moses. Discouragement led from emotionalism and blasphemy to rebellion. Things were coming apart at every seam. "It's the leader's fault," they said. How many churches have crumbled because people lost their focus on God's power and, before you could snap your fingers, they were wanting to dump the pastor?

Let's stop blaming our unbelief on the pastor we once had, on our childhood, on circumstances, or on anything else. There is no excuse for us not to believe in the Lord. Christ is still challenging us as he did Peter on the lake one night. Even though Peter was walking on the water, "when he saw the wind, he was afraid and, beginning to sink, cried out, 'Lord, save me!' Immediately Jesus reached out his hand and caught him. 'You of little faith,' he said, 'why did you doubt?'" (Matthew 14:30–31).

FAITH FOR THE LONG HAUL

NOW WE FINALLY SEE why the Bible so many times holds up the great value of *endurance*. That virtue is not often mentioned in our day. We lean more toward spectacular things like great preaching and dynamic spiritual gifts. But the persistent faith that holds onto God, enduring all the various situations of life no matter how difficult—*that* is something we need to ask God for more and more.

Vincent and Daphne Rodriguez are the kind of steady, salt-of-the-earth people whom every pastor loves to have in a congregation. They live in Queens; he has been a reliable letter carrier for the Postal Service his whole life, while she has been a dedicated homemaker for their three children.

While he was volunteering at a children's camp in the Catskill Mountains one summer, Vincent's heart was touched by the boys and girls he met who didn't have fathers. He and Daphne talked about the children's obvious needs for love and care. In time, the Rodriguezes, then in their early forties, applied to the Salvation Army to become foster parents.

They had hardly finished their training when, a few days before Christmas 1988, the phone rang at one o'clock in the morning. A pitiful baby girl in Beth-Israel Hospital—born more than a month prematurely and addicted through her mother to crack cocaine, heroin, and morphine—needed a home. She had finally gotten up to five pounds in weight and could now be released to foster care. Her mother was a young addict who was clearly unfit to care for her, living most of the time in the streets as a prostitute. Would Vincent and Daphne take the baby?

"We didn't know anything about addiction in infants," says Daphne, like her husband a quiet person. "We had assumed we'd probably be getting a healthy child who was perhaps just from a poor economic environment. Without knowing what we were walking into, we said yes."

By ten o'clock the next evening, two social workers were on their doorstep with a bundle in blankets. For the next twenty-four hours, the Rodriguez family did little else but hover in a circle around the child and admire her! When she cried, which was often, they would pass her from one set of arms to the next. "We felt so sorry for her," says Vincent. "She was our surprise gift for Christmas, and we were happy that God had brought her our way."

But the girl didn't quite look like a normal baby, for the stress of drug withdrawal seemed etched upon her tiny face. At the church, she was dedicated to the Lord in a Sunday afternoon service when she was two months old—and weighed six pounds. I broke down as I held her up to the Lord, and the congregation adopted her as their own.

In the Rodriguez home, life was settling into the realities of taking care of a very disturbed newborn. She twitched and jerked and cried out constantly in the pain of withdrawal. Daphne had prepared herself for middle-of-the-night feedings, of course, but she was hardly expecting to be up every two hours, preparing more milk to calm the baby's frazzled nervous system. She would pace the floor, holding the baby tight to give a feeling of security. As the weeks wore on, this was turning into more of an ordeal than Daphne had bargained for. And yet they felt that God had led them to take this child.

"I kept telling myself that God had his hand on her, because he had allowed her to live, even though she was only two-and-a-half pounds at birth," Daphne says. "She hadn't even been given a name. So we chose one ourselves; at our teenage daughter's suggestion, we picked out a beautiful Bible name, Hannah."

Daphne figured out that if she put her teenagers in charge of the baby each afternoon when they came home from school, she could get at least a nap in order to fortify herself for the next night ahead. Otherwise, an hour of sleep at a time was the best she could hope for. Even Vincent's sleep was disrupted.

"But even in the times I was exhausted or didn't feel well myself, I kept going," Daphne remembers. "I tried to soothe her with Christian music through the day. One particular recording—'I Exalt Thee' by Phil Driscoll—seemed to calm her shaking in the bassinet. We played it every day, and the crying would stop."

When I would see them in church and ask how it was going, Daphne would just sort of shrug as she said, "Pastor, it's really hard! She needs me all night long, it seems; I can't get any sleep." I felt concerned for them, and more than once I asked the congregation to continue to bring the Rodriguezes' situation to God at the throne of grace.

In time, Hannah's health improved. She gained weight. At the end of the first year, she finally began sleeping through the night. Her crawling and walking came later than usual, but that was to be expected. So was her hyperactivity.

With a steady diet of love and prayer, Hannah developed into a toddler. Looking ahead toward the school years, however, Daphne saw trouble. Would this child be able to sit still and learn? She had Hannah tested for attention deficit disorder, and that led to placement in a special education program from age three-and-a-half to five. The program had the additional benefit of giving the tired mother a much-needed break from the daily vigil.

When Hannah reached five years of age, Vincent and Daphne formally adopted her. The ink was hardly dry on the adoption decree, making them permanently responsible for Hannah, when a whole new problem erupted. Hannah developed a cold that she couldn't seem to shake; her face became very dry and blotchy. The condition hung on until finally Daphne took her to the doctor and requested a full physical examination. Two days later, a nurse called: "You need to come back for a consultation."

"Why?" Daphne asked. "What's wrong?"

"Well, something is showing here that doesn't look right. The enzymes in her liver are way too high. We need to run these tests again."

Soon the truth came out: The little girl, having already fought off addiction to hard drugs from her birth mother, was also afflicted with hepatitis C—a serious disease that saps energy, sometimes turns the eyes and skin yellow, and wastes away the liver over time.

"Oh, God—how can this be?" Daphne cried. "After all we've been through with Hannah already—why wasn't this discovered back when she was born?"

So many questions, so few answers. Discouragement swept over the besieged family. When they told me the bad news, I realized that a new battle of faith for Hannah had begun for all of us at the church.

We enlisted the efforts of the Brooklyn Tabernacle Prayer Band (a group that intercedes around the clock, seven days a week), the members of the choir, and everyone else we could. We agreed together that God had created this child and had brought her through all the terrors of drug withdrawal, and we now stood united in faith against this latest threat. "God must be planning to use her for something great," we said.

In time, with the help of the Salvation Army, the Rodriguezes secured the help of a chief specialist at Schneider Children's Hospital, part of the Long Island Jewish medical complex, who took on Hannah's case. He put her on a regimen of medication to fight the disease. Vincent even steeled himself to give his daughter injections, which were required three times a week for the next eighteen months. Hannah's condition stabilized.

Throughout the primary grades, Hannah struggled to keep up with her learning. Daphne was a frequent face in the school hallways, working with the teachers to find solutions for her little girl. Performance gradually improved. They never gave up, no matter what new obstacle appeared. They just refused to stop fighting for Hannah.

Today Hannah's hepatitis C is in remission, and her medications have been dropped. She is a beautiful girl with a lovely round face and a shy smile. "We are just trusting in the Lord that he is healing her completely," Vincent says.

"What a testimony she will be able to give in years to come. I sometimes tell my daughter, 'Someday you will get to stand on the highest building in the city and tell everybody!' She always smiles when I say that, and I do, too. The miracle is on its way."

STAY THE COURSE

THE APOSTLE PAUL KNEW that this kind of spiritual endurance was vital for his own spiritual children. He told them that he never stopped praying for them to be "strengthened with all power according to his glorious might so that you may have great endurance and patience, and joyfully giving thanks to the Father" (Colossians 1:11). He brought them tenderly to God in prayer, that they might be able to keep on keeping on, no matter what attacks were made upon their faith.

Many sensational gifts and talents don't mean much over the long haul. The longer I live, the more I treasure people who just keep walking with God. They aren't up or down, left or right; they're always steady on the course, praising God and believing his Word.

> **Many sensational gifts and talents don't mean much over the long haul. The longer I live, the more I treasure people who just keep walking with God.** ~

Just as our bodies need strength in order to keep functioning, our spirits need endurance. When our faith becomes weakened through discouragement, we have trouble standing on God's promises. We struggle to say no to temptation.

It's easy to give in to the devil. "The Big D" threatens to snuff out our spiritual life. But with God, we can have the power to resist discouragement. He can give us the spirit of Caleb and Joshua that triumphs despite the difficulties facing us.

Notice that Paul *prays* for endurance. This was not something he could transmit by verbal teaching to the Colossian believers. This wonderful strength had to come directly from God at the throne of grace.

And it will *keep* coming as we *keep* asking and trusting in our God.

NINE

~

Grace That
Is Greater

Many times at the end of our services, I meet people at the altar who are so ashamed that they often will not even look me in the eye. Their shoulders are slumped; their gaze is on the carpet. I sense no faith in them to ask Christ for mercy. Praise and worship seem impossible. They are living under the heavy burden of their own failure, with no hope that their life can be retrieved. They now feel too unworthy to expect any blessings from a holy and righteous God.

I am not just talking about people with the stereotypical inner-city problems of drugs, prostitution, or whatever. These are average-looking people who have simply given in to a besetting sin so often that they are convinced they will never rise above it.

Often, as the congregation is worshiping in the background with a song such as "Grace, grace, God's grace— grace that will pardon and cleanse within," I notice that the person before me isn't singing along. It is because the person isn't sure that the song could really be true for him or her. Sometimes I will gently try to lift the person's chin or perhaps the hands in upward openness to God.

How I love to remind these people of someone in the Bible whose life story is often forgotten. You might not think of him as a failure, because his name, in fact, shows up in very good company. One place is on the very first page of the New Testament, where the opening lines say,

A record of the genealogy of Jesus Christ the son of David, the son of Abraham:

Abraham was the father of Isaac,
 Isaac the father of Jacob,
 Jacob the father of *Judah* and his brothers,
 Judah the father of Perez and Zerah, whose mother
  was Tamar (Matthew 1:1–3).

How nice and orderly. This passage sets down a clear track from Abraham, the father of the Jewish nation, to Jesus, so that everyone in the first century would know that this Messiah was honest-to-goodness Jewish. Along the way, that track runs straight through Judah and his family.

Then, on one of the last pages of the New Testament, the apostle John writes,

I saw in the right hand of him who sat on the throne a scroll with writing on both sides and sealed with seven seals. And I saw a mighty angel proclaiming in a loud voice, "Who is worthy to break the seals and open the scroll?" But no one in heaven or on earth or under the earth could open the scroll or even look inside it. I wept and wept because no one was found who was worthy to open the scroll or look inside. Then one of the elders said to me, "Do not weep! See, the Lion of the tribe of *Judah*, the Root of David, has triumphed. He is able to open the scroll and its seven seals" (Revelation 5:1–5).

How wonderful that while many others were disqualified, someone who came from the tribe of Judah met the standard to open the mysteries of God. That someone, of course, was Jesus Christ.

This Judah must have been quite a godly man, right? Of all of Jacob's twelve sons, only he is mentioned in the genealogy of Christ. The other eleven were passed over by God. At the climax of history in heaven, it is Judah's offspring who is hailed as worthy when all others fail the test. When we get to heaven someday, we will no doubt continue to hear Judah's name often.

But what do you really know about this man Judah?

A SORDID TALE

JUDAH GETS A WHOLE chapter of the Bible to himself—Genesis 38—and that is the best place to get acquainted with him. If you have the stomach for it, that is. (You might not want to read this chapter aloud to your children in family devotions.)

The story begins with Judah drifting away from the rest of the family and marrying a Canaanite woman (vv. 1–2). That was his first mistake. His uncle, Esau, had already been down that road, getting into a mess by marrying outside of those who served the one true God (see Genesis 26:34–35). As a result, Judah's grandparents had gone to great lengths to make sure their other son, Jacob, didn't make the same error. They told him in no uncertain terms to avoid Canaanite women (Genesis 28:1) and sent him on a long trip to find the right kind of wife.

But Judah disregarded their counsel entirely. He married "the daughter of a Canaanite man named Shua" (Genesis 38:2). The children born to them apparently grew up getting mixed messages about the true God versus Canaan's idols. The bad results showed up quickly in the first son, who turned out to be so wicked that the Lord put him to death in early adulthood (v. 7).

That left behind a young widow named Tamar. Judah asked his second son to marry her, as was the social requirement in those days. But the son selfishly refused. Because of this, God brought destruction on him also.

Judah now procrastinated about giving his third son, Shelah, to Tamar. The years went by, and Tamar kept waiting. She was getting past her prime, and she was lonely. Finally, she heard about a trip her father-in-law, Judah, was going to take. It was sheep-shearing time, which was payday for those in the sheep business. Money flowed and people partied. To Tamar, this seemed like the perfect opportunity to carry out a terrible plan. She covered her face with some kind of shawl and posed along the road as a prostitute.

The Bible records that Judah, "not realizing that she was his daughter-in-law, ... went over to her by the roadside and said, 'Come now, let me sleep with you'" (v. 16). Judah paid for her services, but it resulted in Tamar's becoming pregnant with twins. Judah went home none the wiser.

When the news came out that Tamar was having a baby, Judah threw a righteous fit. How dare his daughter-in-law cause disgrace on the family! "Bring her out and have her burned to death!" he stormed (v. 24).

As she was being dragged out into the public square, she calmly identified her sexual partner by holding up the personal property Judah had left with her as a down payment for her services. Judah was humiliated before all and had to admit, "She is more righteous than I" (v. 26).

DISQUALIFIED?

YOU JUST WANT TO shield your eyes from this kind of ugliness, don't you? It sounds like something in the *National Enquirer.* If you or I have an ancestor in our families who did something like this, we don't talk about it. We probably leave his picture out of the family album. We don't bring up his name to our children—and hope they never ask. People who so mess up their lives—and others' lives—are best left unmentioned.

Why would God put this seamy story in the Bible? It doesn't seem fit for print. Or, if God had to include the story, why didn't he then say to us, "The stern lesson of this is that the lineage of my holy Son will be Abraham—Isaac—Jacob—*Benjamin*," or one of the other sons? After all, hadn't Judah thoroughly disqualified himself?

Left to our own devices, any of us can self-destruct within an hour, just as Judah did. "There is no one righteous, not even one" (Romans 3:10). "We all, like sheep, have gone astray, each of us has turned to his own way" (Isaiah 53:6). "I know that nothing good lives in me, that is, in my sinful nature" (Romans 7:18). Thus, there is no need for self-righteous snickering as we read Judah's story.

> **We all can be self-righteous and pompous. If every moment of our past were put on the big screen at church, who of us would seem so wonderful?** ∾

God has given clear testimony about our moral standing with him. But unfortunately, we are very good at condemning others for the very things we also do. "So-and-so in the church is selfish ... so-and-so is racist ... so-and-so is a hypocrite." But somehow, the mirror doesn't work for us.

Like Judah when he was told about his daughter-in-law's pregnancy, we can all be self-righteous and pompous. Not only are we weak, but we are judgmental on top of it! Wouldn't it be better to stop giving opinions about everyone else and do a better job of humbly looking after our own hearts? If every moment of our past were put on the big screen at church, who of us would seem so wonderful?

My main concern today is that we have lost sight of the reason God included Judah's ugly story in the Bible. We are drifting away from the New Testament's message of God's amazing grace to change and redeem soiled people; instead, we are moralizing and expressing self-righteous disdain over the horrible lives others are living around us. Instead of exalting Jesus, who came as a spiritual physician for the sick and unlovely, we are busy rehearsing all the commandments of God, as if that alone would change a single soul. We are giving people only the law, when what they crave is the love and grace of God.

We have forgotten that God specializes in cases such as Judah. We should return to preaching boldly what Paul wrote to the Corinthians—not stopping two-thirds of the way through the paragraph, but continuing on to the glorious end:

> Do you not know that the wicked will not inherit the kingdom of God? Do not be deceived: Neither the sexually immoral nor idolaters nor adulterers nor male prostitutes nor homosexual offenders nor thieves nor the greedy nor drunkards nor slanderers nor swindlers will inherit the kingdom of God. *And that is what some of you were. But you were washed, you were sanctified, you were justified in the name of the Lord Jesus Christ and by the Spirit of our God* (1 Corinthians 6:9–11).

The early Christian church had its own share of "Judahs," but "where sin increased, grace increased all the more" (Romans 5:20).

GRACE BEYOND REASON

THE DEVIL'S SPECIALTY is to swarm in on people and hiss, "You did it! You really messed up! If people only knew. . . . You're not what you seem to be. Do you think you're going to get away with this?" And the devil's victims hardly feel like living. They feel unworthy to go to church. They avoid their Bibles. They see no hope of change.

Satan wants to hide the fact that the mercy of God is for *everyone* who has messed up. As high as the heavens are above the earth, so are God's ways higher than ours (Isaiah 55:9). He delights in mercy. James writes, "Mercy triumphs over judgment" (2:13). God's specialty is forgiving and putting away people's sins from his sight. He delights in taking failures such as Judah and weaving them into the ancestry of his own Son, Jesus Christ.

What is even more remarkable is this: The genealogy of Jesus in Matthew 1:3 continues through Judah and then goes *not* to his legitimate son, Shelah—but to Perez, Tamar's boy, the child of incest. How incredible! It is as if God were saying, "Forever I want my people to know that I not only forgive mess-ups, but I can take them and touch them and heal them—and put them in the line that leads to Christ." What Satan means for evil, God is able to change and work out for good (Genesis 50:20).

To this very day, God delights in hearing Judah's name echo through the heavenly halls. He takes sinners like you and me and makes us right. He takes dirt and pollution and transforms them into holiness. He takes the crooked thing and makes it straight. He takes the tangles of our lives and weaves something new, so that we emerge singing Hallelujah. We love God, not because we've been so good, but because *he* is so good, and his mercy endures forever.

The Lion of the tribe of Judah is about deliverance, not condemnation. He takes our mistakes and wanderings and redeems them for his glory. Greater than his glory as Creator and Sustainer of the universe is the glory of his grace to losers like you and me. No record is so stained, no case so hopeless that he cannot reach down and bring salvation to that person.

....

God takes sinners like you and me and makes us right. He takes dirt and pollution and transforms them into holiness. He takes the crooked thing and makes it straight. ❧

....

One of the outstanding gospel singers in America today is a trophy of that kind of divine mercy. When audiences listen to Calvin Hunt's soaring tenor voice, they can hardly imagine that at one time he virtually destroyed his body with crack cocaine—and ravaged the lives of his wife and two stepchildren as well. His story is more than just self-destruction through drugs; it spreads its pain to the single mom he had rescued in the aftermath of her abusive first marriage, and to her innocent daughter and son.

Calvin met the trim, attractive Miriam and her two preschoolers when he was just twenty years old. Miriam lived in the apartment two floors below his mother, and she and Calvin warmed to each other right away. Little Monique and Freddy liked the handsome young construction worker with the hard hat who made them laugh. Calvin was also something of a weekend musician, playing guitar and singing in nightclubs.

Miriam's divorce was not yet final, and Calvin had to comfort her more than once after she had been beaten up by her estranged husband. On one occasion, when the man knocked her out cold, Calvin took Miriam to the emergency room. Their relationship flourished over the next year and then even survived a one-year army stint by Calvin that took him away from New York City.

"When I came back home," Calvin admits, "the easiest thing for me to do was just to move in with her. I went back to working road construction, and we had enough money to party through the weekends." The couple eventually added snorting cocaine to their fairly heavy drinking as they and their friends sought new thrills. Then they added marijuana to the mix, sometimes even sprinkling the joints with cocaine before rolling them in order to experience both drugs at once.

The live-in arrangement continued with little change, until five years later when Miriam told Calvin they ought to get married. And so in 1984, they wed.

SOMETHING NEW

ONE NIGHT THE BEST man from their wedding invited them to a party at his home that featured something new: "freebasing" cocaine, or heating it and smoking it through a glass bottle. Calvin was intrigued; he asked his friend for a hit. But the new drug didn't seem to have much effect, Calvin thought. Miriam gave it a try as well, with minimal results.

Or so they thought. Not until they left the friend's apartment at 7:30 the next morning, having been awake all night and having spent Calvin's entire $720 paycheck for the week, did they realize they had discovered something powerfully attractive—and deadly. They had now joined the world of crack cocaine.

"I remember us going back home, and I just felt horrible the whole weekend," Calvin says. "By the time I went to work on Monday, I was lecturing myself about being more responsible. I had a family to support, and I needed to get back in control.

"Would you believe that by the next Friday night when I cashed my check, I called Miriam and told her to get the kids ready for bed early, because I'd be bringing home 'the stuff'? I showed up with all the new paraphernalia, ready for action. I prepared the crack over the kitchen stove just as I'd seen my friend do it the week before, and again the two of us were up all night. By the time the sun came up Saturday morning, we had gone through another whole paycheck."

This pattern endured for eight months. Meanwhile, household bills went unpaid, the children lacked warm winter clothing, and the rent fell behind. Miriam's brothers, who were Christians, urged her to stop destroying herself, but neither she nor Calvin would listen.

> **If Calvin had any spare cash in his pocket, it went for crack. If he didn't have cash, he would manufacture some by stealing the battery or tires from a parked car to resell.** ~

Calvin's obsession with drugs grew ever stronger, and not just on the weekends. If he had any spare cash in his pocket, it went for crack. If he didn't have cash, he would manufacture some by stealing the tires or the battery from a parked car to resell. Some nights he didn't come home at all.

Obviously, Calvin's job performance suffered. One day his boss pulled Calvin aside for a talk. There were tears in the man's eyes as he said quietly, "You've been one of my most valued employees. I don't know what's happening, and I don't want to know—but whatever it is, you better get it fixed, because you're about to lose your job."

The truth was, Calvin had a new superboss in his life: crack. "I began losing a lot of weight," Calvin says. "I'd be gone three, four, even five days at a time—spending my life in crack dens. Yes, I had a home and a wife and two children—but when I was doing crack, home was the last place I wanted to be.

"The people I did drugs with were actually a pretty scary bunch—violent and heartless. But as long as I was high, I didn't even notice that."

Betrayed

Miriam grew increasingly concerned. What was happening to the man she loved, her one-time knight in shining armor? Hadn't she already been through enough chaos with her first husband—and now this? One night she looked at her two children sleeping innocently in bed while Calvin and his friends were in the kitchen getting high. Moral principles once learned long ago seemed to rise up to warn her of where this was all heading. She promptly threw all the guys out—including Calvin.

Miriam began to see that she was being terribly betrayed by a man for the second time in her life. The first one had beaten her physically; the second one was hurting her and her children even more painfully with his addiction. Like Judah of old, he was wreaking tremendous damage on his family through his unbridled thrill-seeking.

"I pleaded with him to stop," says Miriam. "I said, 'Calvin, this is going to kill us! It's going to destroy our marriage.' The arguments got so bad that sometimes I had to have him escorted out of the house. My son began studying ways to add more locks to the apartment so Calvin couldn't get back in."

At the very time Calvin was deserting the family, Miriam put her faith in Christ. Her spiritual life deepened, and her prayer life increased. She found a church and would openly ask for the prayers of others to bring her husband back from the brink. She refused to contemplate the other options: separation, divorce, or his untimely death. She simply believed that God would somehow rescue their family.

She even began to tell Calvin, "God is going to set you free—I just know it!" Of course, that made him furious. He also got irked at the Brooklyn Tabernacle Choir music she had begun to play. She loved it and would respond in worship, sometimes even weeping for joy as she praised the Lord. Calvin would snap back, "If that stuff makes you cry, why don't you turn it off?" He would sometimes fling the cassette out the window, but his wife would quickly replace it.

One day young Monique found a flyer announcing a Friday night showing of the film *A Cry for Freedom*, being sponsored in a high school auditorium by Christ Tabernacle in Queens. The twelve-year-old insisted that Dad go with them to see it. He brushed her off.

Suddenly something rose up within the girl. She said, "Daddy, remember all the neat things we used to do together? We don't do anything anymore. You know what—it's all about you and that drug, whatever it is! Your problem is, you're hooked, and you won't admit it!"

Calvin flared back. "You shut up! Keep talking like that, and I'll give you a whipping!"

"Go ahead, Daddy!" the brave girl responded. "You can beat me and stomp on me if you want—but when you're finished, you'll still be hooked on that stuff." At that, she ran out of the kitchen.

Calvin picked up the flyer from the table. He looked at the sketch of a man inside the bottle that is used for smoking crack, his hands pressed against the glass with a desperate look on his face. Calvin's heart melted enough that he reluctantly agreed to attend the showing.

At the last minute, Calvin tried to back out, but without success. The film's story line turned out to be a shockingly close replica of the Hunts themselves: a husband addicted to crack, and his formerly addicted wife now praying for his deliverance. When the pastor gave an invitation at the end, Calvin was the first one kneeling at the altar. "I didn't actually ask Jesus to come into my heart," he says, "but I was just so guilt-ridden that I had to at least pray and admit the pain I was causing everyone. I started to cry. Miriam and the kids came alongside, and we all cried together."

The next Sunday, the family returned to church, and while Miriam and the children were overjoyed, Calvin still was not willing to get serious about the Lord. *God can't do anything for me*, he told himself. *What am I doing here?* By the next weekend, he was on the run again.

BEARING DOWN

NOW THE CHURCH BODY began to pray harder for Calvin Hunt's salvation. Calvin learned to time his visits back to the apartment during the hours when he knew everyone would be at church. He would sneak in to get a fresh supply of clean clothes and then quickly leave.

"I knew that Calvin was in a prison," says Miriam. "Being an ex-addict myself—I had done heroin before I ever met him—I knew the unbelievable power of this kind of substance. That's why I prayed so hard, crying out to God to set him free, and got all my friends to pray with me. Every mealtime prayer with my kids, every bedtime prayer included, 'O God, please set Daddy free!'"

Another three years went by. Calvin got worse instead of better. At one point he was actually sleeping in a large doghouse in someone's backyard rather than going home to his own bed. He was seriously dehydrated, his cheeks sunken, giving him the wasted look so common among addicts. With no money, Miriam and the children had to apply for food stamps and Medicaid.

Finally, one night—the same night as Christ Tabernacle's weekly prayer meeting—Calvin headed once again for the family apartment after his wife and children had left. In the quietness he found some food in the refrigerator, then took a shower and put on clean clothes. There was still time for a short nap, so he decided to lie down.

But for some reason, he couldn't sleep. Soon he heard a noise. From a closet came the soft sound of someone weeping! He sat up. Maybe Miriam and the children were home after all.

He looked in the children's rooms, under the beds, inside the various closets. No one! But the sobbing continued. He stood in the living room and said out loud, "I know you guys are in here—come on out!" Nobody appeared.

Calvin thought of lying down once again, but something inside him seemed to say, *If you go to sleep tonight, you'll never wake up again.* He panicked. ～

Now Calvin was spooked. He thought of lying down once again, but something inside him seemed to say, *If you go to sleep tonight, you'll never wake up again.* He panicked. Running out the door, he dashed three blocks to the train station to go see if his wife and children were really at the prayer meeting or not.

He burst into the church and stood at the back of the center aisle, scanning the crowd. Suddenly the same sounds of crying struck his ears—only much louder than back in the apartment. The whole congregation was in earnest prayer, calling out *his* name to God in faith! Calvin was thunderstruck as he slowly moved down the aisle, gazing at the people's upraised hands and their eyes tightly shut in prayer, tears running down their faces. "O God, wherever Calvin Hunt is, bring him to this building!" they pleaded. "Don't let this family go through this horror another day. Lord, you are able! Set him free from his bondage once and for all!"

Soon Calvin found himself at the front, directly before the pulpit. The pastor in charge opened his eyes, took one glance—and then gazed upward toward heaven as he said into the microphone, "Thank you, Lord! Thank you, Jesus! Here he is!"

With that, the congregation went absolutely crazy. They had been calling upon the Lord to bring Calvin to himself, and it was happening right before their very eyes.

Falling to his knees, Calvin burst into uncontrollable sobs. Miriam and the children came from their pew to huddle around him as he prayed, "O God, I've become everything I said I'd never be. I don't want to die this way. Please come into my life and set me free. Oh, Jesus, I need you so much!"

That summer night in 1988 was the turning point for Calvin Hunt. Says Miriam, "It was almost as if he had walked slowly down the center aisle of the church as in a wedding, to be married to Christ. Jesus was patiently waiting for him at the altar. No wonder we all burst into tears!"

ON A NEW KIND OF ROAD

THE OLD LIFE and old patterns put up some resistance for Calvin, to be sure, but the pastors of Christ Tabernacle spoke very straight to him about getting into a Christian residential program in Pennsylvania called Youth Challenge. He agreed to go.

Six months later, Calvin returned to New York City, strong in his faith and ready to live for God. He managed to get his old road construction job back. My wife and I saw him several nights with his crew out working on the Brooklyn-Queens Expressway as we were driving home after church. He was so happy in the Lord! Soon he began turning his singing talent to godly purposes.

Once in a restaurant, Calvin got up to go to the men's room, and there in a stall was someone smoking crack! All of the old desires began to tug at him, but he quickly prayed. *God, I need you to help me right now!* He steadied himself. When the man appeared, Calvin looked him in the eye and said, "Let me tell you something from experience: That stuff is going to destroy your life."

"Whatcha talkin' 'bout, man?"

"I'm serious. It will destroy you—but Jesus can help you overcome it."

The next thing Calvin did was head straight for a telephone to call Miriam and report his victory at overcoming temptation. They rejoiced together in the new strength God had given.

Today Calvin Hunt no longer wields a jackhammer on the highways of New York City. He has recorded two gospel albums and travels full-time, telling audiences nationwide about the road to God's power in their lives. He is also a featured soloist with our choir—the group he once despised—

and a member of the sixteen-voice Brooklyn Tabernacle Singers. Wherever he goes, people's hearts are lifted in praise for God's victory in his life.

Instead of destroying his family, Calvin is now its godly leader—including two new children that the Lord has graciously given to him and Miriam. Doctors had led them to believe that they had both so abused their bodies that conception was unlikely. Then came a daughter named Mia and, a couple of years later, a son named Calvin Jr. From the sin and hopelessness that seemed ready to swallow Calvin and Miriam, God has raised up another monument to the saving power of Jesus Christ, the Lion of the tribe of Judah.

> **May God deliver us from self-righteous judging and make us, instead, merciful carriers of Christ's salvation and freedom everywhere we go.** ~

Let us spread the message far and wide: Jesus Christ is mighty to save! No matter how ruined the life, his blood can erase the darkest stain, and his Spirit can breathe new life into fallen men and women. He is the God of Judah—the man who was a moral failure, a hypocrite, and a disgrace to God and his family. But through Judah we see more clearly the depth of the Lord's love and the incredible richness of his mercy.

May God deliver us from self-righteous judging and make us, instead, merciful carriers of Christ's salvation and freedom everywhere we go. Jesus "came into the world to save sinners," the apostle Paul wrote, even considering himself to be "the worst" of the lot (1 Timothy 1:15). But rejoice in why he was so candid about his condition, for it applies to us also: "For that very reason I was shown mercy so that in me, the worst of sinners, Christ Jesus might display his unlimited patience as an example for those who would believe on him and receive eternal life. Now to the King eternal, immortal, invisible, the only God, be honor and glory for ever and ever. Amen" (vv. 16–17).

PART 3

~

Following the
Divine Channel

TEN

~

Father of
the Faithful

HAVE YOU EVER READ in Scripture about "Father David"?

Or "Father Moses"?

What about "Father Daniel"?

These were all mighty men of God, to be sure. They rank among the greatest warriors, kings, prophets, and leaders of sacred history. But none of them achieved the special honor bestowed upon "the father of all who believe, ... the father of [those] who also walk in the footsteps of faith, ... our father in the sight of God, in whom he believed, ... the father of many nations" (Romans 4:11–12, 17–18). His name is Abraham.

We know that Jesus once disputed using the title *father* in reference to any mortal human (see Matthew 23:9). Yet, when the apostle Paul came to write the fourth chapter of Romans, it sounds almost as if he couldn't help himself. *Abraham ... oh, my ... he's the very symbol of living by faith ... I have to set him preeminent above all others ... he's the spiritual father of all who believe God's promises.*

This Abraham was obviously the great example when it comes to faith. How did he ever develop such towering trust in God?

HE LIVED BY PROMISES, NOT COMMANDS

ON THAT EPIC DAY when God first spoke to Abram (as he was then known), God said,

> Leave your country, your people and your father's household and go to the land I will show you.
>
> I will make you into a great nation
>   and I will bless you;
> I will make your name great,
>   and you will be a blessing.
> I will bless those who bless you,
>   and whoever curses you I will curse;
> and all peoples on earth
>   will be blessed through you (Genesis 12:1–3).

God directed Abram to do only one thing—"Leave"—and in return, God would do eight wonderful things for him. That number alone speaks of the graciousness and goodness of God.

But it did require Abram to leave his country, his people, and his relatives—in other words, his comfort zone. He had to give up the land he knew best, the culture he had grown up in, the familiar sights and sounds. People who walk by faith often hear God's voice telling them, "You need to leave now. It's time to move on to something new."

Sometimes that word has to do with geography, as in Abram's case. We are currently experiencing this at the Brooklyn Tabernacle as we get ready to leave our present building, where we have been since 1979, and head for the larger downtown theater where we believe God is sending us. We have bought this massive shell, built in 1914, even though as I'm writing this we still do not know how we will raise the millions needed for renovation. We are having to walk by faith.

At other times, God directs his people to leave certain work situations, sever pleasant relationships, or make other difficult changes. When you walk by faith, God never lets you settle into some plateau. Just when you reach a certain place spiritually and decide to pitch your tent and relax for the rest of your life, God says, "Leave." This was the story of Abram. In fact, he was never allowed to settle down permanently as long as he lived.

> **When you walk by faith, God never lets you settle into some plateau.** ⌒

But we don't have to be afraid. God in the same breath can begin to inundate us with promises, as he did Abram. See the great things the Lord vowed to do:

1. "... the land I will show you." In other words, God will point out the destination.
2. "I will make you into a great nation."
3. "I will bless you."
4. "I will make your name great."
5. "You will be a blessing."
6. "I will bless those who bless you."
7. "Whoever curses you I will curse."
8. "All peoples on earth will be blessed through you."

Thus, Abram's family caravan left town in a mode of *living off the promises of God.* That was their source, and it must be ours as well. We cannot live off the commands of God, but rather the promises. The commands of God reveal his holy character to us, but they hold no accompanying power. Instead, the grace of God flows through the channel of his promises. God must first do for us what he promised, and only then will we be able to walk in obedience to his commands. Remember, he is our Source—everything must start from him.

It is true that God's moral commands teach us where we fall short. That is necessary—but it doesn't bring a solution to our human dilemma. Only the promises bring us hope, if we respond in faith, as Abram did. That is what sustained him throughout his life. By the time Abram arrived in Canaan, God was already adding more promises to the original group. He said, "To your offspring I will give this land" (v. 7). His abundance kept flowing.

But the great majority of us are command-oriented. Every day we wake up conscious of God's moral law and try to do right so he will approve of us at the end of the day. Yet this is a great struggle. We would do far better to wake up thinking about God's wonderful promises—what he has said he will do for us today. Then his power working in us will tenderly direct us in the way of obedience and right living.

> **God's moral commands teach us where we fall short. That is necessary—but only the *promises* bring us hope, if we respond in faith.** ～

The tender love of God toward us, as revealed in his gracious promises, is the only thing that draws us to a closer walk with the Lord. Righteous commands alone, and the judgment always linked to them, can easily frighten us away. Martin Luther was originally repelled by the holy God he saw as only making demands and sentencing people to judgment. Then he saw the truth "the righteous will live by faith" (Romans 1:17). This spoke of grace and mercy to all who simply believe God. Out of this came the whole Protestant Reformation, which turned the world upside down.

Abram felt so close to God that "he built an altar to the LORD and called on the name of the LORD" (Genesis 12:8) there between the towns of Bethel and Ai. Abram's heart reached out to God in worship. This God had been so good to him, so generous, so affirming. Abram had not earned any promise or blessing by previous conduct; it was all because of grace. He could not help lifting up his heart and hands to God in adoration.

HE HAD NO MASTER PLAN

THE BOOK OF HEBREWS tells us that "by faith Abraham . . . obeyed and went, even though he did not know where he was going" (11:8). He had no map, no AAA brochure, no lineup of motel reservations along the way. His caravan simply headed west toward the Mediterranean, and that was that. God had said he would show him where to stop sometime in the future when he got to wherever he was going.

You and I would struggle with this, wouldn't we? Not only in our vacation travel, but in guiding our careers and our churches, we simply have to have a comprehensive plan. I hear pastors say all the time, "Let's see, regarding this or that outreach—will it pay? Is it going to be cost-effective? How can I be sure it will work? Will everyone be pleased?" We do very few things by faith.

Abram didn't have a clue. If you had met up with his caravan at some oasis, the conversation might have gone like this:

"Mr. Abram, where are you going?"

"I don't know."

"Well, how will you know when you get there?"

"I don't know that, either. God only said he would show me."

"You have quite an entourage here. When you do arrive, who will supply all the food you'll need? After all, if you're going to survive in a new place, how are you going to eat"?

"I don't know. He just said he would take care of me."

"You don't seem to have a security force. Who is going to protect you from the Jebusites, the Hittites, the Amorites, and all the rest of the warring tribes?"

Abram would just shake his head and wander away.

Faith is happy to step out not knowing where it's going so long as it knows Who is going along. As long as God's strong hand was holding Abram's, everything was going to work out just fine. The caravan moved ahead in faith.

> **Faith is happy to step out not knowing where it's going so long as it knows Who is going along.** ~

We like to control the map of our life and know everything well in advance. But faith is content just knowing that God's promise cannot fail. This, in fact, is the excitement of walking with God. When we read the book of Acts, we never quite know what's going to happen with the next turn of the page. The Spirit is in control, and that is enough. Paul had no formula as to how he would evangelize; he was simply going by faith. God unveiled the route as he went along.

I was invited to speak at a huge conference of pastors where the entire meeting was plotted out, minute by minute. The man who called me graciously explained, "First there will be an opening song, and then one of our denominational leaders will speak for fourteen minutes on a doctrinal topic. Then will come some additional music, and then we'd like you to speak for twenty minutes. Following your remarks, a choir will present some of your wife's music, and then finally a third speaker will speak for twenty minutes. Then will come the benediction."

This was to occur on a Monday. I thought about the physical drain of leading four services in our own church on Sunday and then right away taking a long plane flight to this conference. Did God want all this travel and expense for such an occasion?

When I hesitated, the man said, "Oh, your book *Fresh Wind, Fresh Fire* has been a great blessing in so many of our churches. We really want you to come."

"Well," I said, "I guess what comes to my mind is this: How many points can an audience remember at one sitting? I mean, you've lined up three speakers, each making important statements. . . . People cannot feel deeply about more than a couple of truths at a time. I think I know the type of speaker you're looking for, but I don't think I'm the man. I'm not really sure that's the best way to minister to thousands of pastors anyway."

"What do you mean?" he replied.

"Well, since you mentioned my book, I have an idea. Why don't you think about scratching some of the program and having a prayer meeting instead? We pastors all need more of God. The general spiritual condition of churches all across America right now is not exactly fervent and prayerful. Divorces are plentiful; young people are falling away; pastors are resigning at record rates—maybe the best thing you could do in your conference is to allocate a block of time just to pray. Why not ask God to open up the heavens and come down? He's the one we really need."

This man graciously replied, "But we don't do those things at our conference."

I said, "I'm not familiar with the traditions of your particular group, but I do see in my Bible where some great promises are given to those who call on the Lord and wait for his blessing."

I finished the call by declining the invitation as politely as I could.

A week later, the phone rang again. "We've decided to adjust the service," the man said. "Why don't you come and bring your wife as well as some others, and you can have plenty of time. You can end the service any way you want."

I felt the Lord opening an important night of ministry. We agreed to make the trip. What a sight it was at the end of that meeting to see thousands of ministers reaching out to the Lord, many of them on their knees, and quite a few with copious tears. "Oh, God, we need you in our churches!" they prayed. "Come and light your fire among us." We were all in the same boat. I wasn't speaking down to them as some outside expert from New York City. I needed to pray the same prayer they were praying. What hope is there for the Brooklyn Tabernacle if we don't pray for God to come by his Spirit and do things we could never do?

The promise at the beginning of the book of Acts is "You will receive power when the Holy Spirit comes upon you" (1:8). No wonder Jesus told the disciples to "wait for the gift my Father promised" (1:4)—just as Abram and his wife Sarai had to wait with expectation for what God had promised them. Having faith in the promise is the key and the only hope for anybody's church, whatever the affiliation.

The great search in too many church circles is not for leaders with the faith of Abram who are willing to trust God wherever he leads, but rather for leaders who are sharp and clever at organizing. We forget that the Christian church was founded in a prayer meeting. It was led in its earliest and most successful years by simple men full of faith and the Holy Spirit. They concentrated not on "the secret of church growth," but on the secret of receiving the power God has promised. Because of their faith, the Lord gave them both power and growth.

> **We forget that the Christian church was founded in a prayer meeting.** ∼

Paul was humble enough to admit to the church at Corinth, "When I came to you, brothers, I did not come with eloquence or superior wisdom as I proclaimed to you the testimony about God.... My message and my preaching were not with wise and persuasive words, but with a demonstration of the Spirit's power, *so that your faith might not rest on men's wisdom, but on God's power*" (1 Corinthians 2:1, 4–5). This approach to ministry and igniting faith in God's people is rare today.

In fact, God has a wonderful plan for all his people. But he doesn't have to tell us much about it if he chooses not to. All he asks is that we take his hand and walk along in faith. He will show us soon enough what should be done.

HE FAILED DRAMATICALLY, BUT REBOUNDED

THE CHALLENGE, as we said earlier, is not just to start out in faith, but to continue to walk in faith. The Bible describes the next painful chapter in Abram's life. Although he had started out so wonderfully, he actually failed God by heading down to Egypt because of a famine. He felt the economic pinch, and he reacted. No Scripture shows him receiving any direction from God about this; he just pulled up stakes and moved.

Whenever we stop living by faith, we start unilaterally doing what we think is smart or what circumstances dictate. We soon find ourselves in a weakened position. We get into trouble quickly.

As they neared the Egyptian border, Abram took one look at his beautiful wife and said, "Sarai, I see some problems down the road. Pharaoh and his men will desire you, and they're going to eliminate me in order to have you. So we'd better lie and say you're my sister instead of my wife."

The little scheme only half-worked. Abram avoided losing his life, but poor Sarai was led away to join the royal harem. What an outrageous and low-life thing to do to your own wife! You can be sure the women in the harem didn't get to just sit around there in the palace having Bible studies. Abram saved his own neck, but risked Sarai's virtue and future.

God was watching this whole mess develop and decided to intervene with judgment.

Now, if anyone deserved punishment, it seems it would have been Abram! He was the rascal here. But instead, "the LORD inflicted serious diseases on Pharaoh and his household" (Genesis 12:17), which quickly led Pharaoh to summon Abram.

Pharaoh's wrath exploded in Abram's face: "What is your problem? Why didn't you tell me this was your wife? Take her and get out of my country—now!"

Imagine this great man of faith getting rebuked by a pagan king—justifiably! What a remarkable lesson that in the life of faith, we can wander from the promises and fail so miserably. Nobody yet has walked the perfect faith life. But the important thing is to get back up and back on track. Abram—

"the father of all who believe"—was not quite down for the count.

He and Sarai scurried back again to the land where they belonged, "to the place between Bethel and Ai where his tent had been earlier and where he had first built an altar. There Abram called on the name of the LORD" (Genesis 13:3–4). It seems he could not rest until he got back to the altar where he had once worshiped God—back to the place where he had stood so faithfully on the promises made to him.

> **Whenever we fail God, it is vital to return
> quickly to an altar of consecration and faith.
> God is waiting for us there.** ∽

Whenever we fail God, it is vital to return quickly to that altar of consecration and faith. God is waiting for us there, like the prodigal's father waiting for his son to return. He looks forward to getting us back on track. The greatness of Abram was not in his moral perfection, but in his getting back to God and believing again.

HE DIDN'T PRESS FOR HIS PRIVILEGES

SOON A QUARREL AROSE between Abram and his nephew Lot, because their cattle and sheep were crowding each other. God had blessed them both (even Abram, after selling his wife down the river!) to the point that a joint livestock operation was no longer practical.

> So Abram said to Lot, "Let's not have any quarreling between you and me, or between your herdsmen and mine, for we are brothers. Is not the whole land before

you? Let's part company. If you go to the left, I'll go to the right; if you go to the right, I'll go to the left" (Genesis 13:8–9).

Lot promptly chose the fertile plain—the best the human eye could see—leaving Abram to try to graze his sheep on the rocky mountainside.

But Abram did not protest. He could have "pulled rank"—after all, he was the senior man here, and the younger fellow had no right to take advantage of him. Instead, Abram showed that when you have faith in God, you know God will take care of you no matter what someone else chooses. Faith lets other people do their thing without getting anxious and worried. It leaves its case in God's hands.

Too many times we worry about who is forgetting us, who is not giving us credit, who is reaping benefits at our expense. We lose touch with the fact that when God "brings one down, he exalts another" (Psalm 75:7). Both in the secular environment and in church work, we are anxious about things that are better left in God's hands. Worry always nips at the heels of faith and tries to drag it down.

> **Faith lets other people do their thing without getting anxious and worried. It leaves its case in God's hands.** ∼

Faith deals with the invisible things of God. It refuses to be ruled by the physical senses. Faith is able to say, "You can do what you like, because I know God is going to take care of me. He has promised to bless me wherever he leads me." Remember that even when every demon in hell stands against us, the God of Abraham remains faithful to all his promises. Jesus Christ can do anything but fail his own people who trust in him.

Why not start afresh today to follow in the footsteps of "Father Abraham"? Begin carefully and prayerfully to search the Scriptures, asking the Holy Spirit to make God's promises come alive to the point where you can live off them, even as Abraham did.

Don't be afraid when you don't know exactly how God will lead and supply for you. Rather, just hold firmly to his hand and walk in faith. There is no need to worry about what the other person might be doing. It really doesn't matter, because God has promised to uphold and defend you.

Finally, if you are someone who has "gone down to Egypt"—walked away from your initial trust and consecration to God—then return right now with all your heart to the Lord. Go back to that altar you once made as a place of worship and surrender to God. He has promised to receive everyone who comes to him through Jesus Christ our Lord. Don't hesitate because of how far away you have strayed or what you did while you were there. Although you cannot see him, the Father watches for you even now, waiting with compassion and love for your return home to him.

ELEVEN

~

God's Deeper Work

WE HAVE SEEN that walking by faith is what brings us into the realm of the supernatural power of God. The Spirit works in us to accomplish things that are impossible to the human understanding. God is indeed omnipotent. He has all power.

Many times, our expectation of that power is slightly misdirected. We are primarily looking for God to show his power in creation, in healing bodies, in supplying employment for his people, in bringing a new baby into the world—and these are all wonderful things. But the Bible declares that the greatest things he does are *internal*, not external. Ephesians 3:20 speaks of God "who is able to do immeasurably more than all we ask or imagine" (we like that part), "according to his power that is at work *within* us."

Only the internal things will go with us into the next world. We won't be dragging along our bodies, our cars, our houses, or our lands. The great church leader Andrew Murray once said, "Your heart is your world, and your world is your heart," and this is the main place where God works in our lives.

What good is it if God heals you and keeps you alive for an extra twenty years if you walk in disobedience for those twenty years? What good is any external blessing without God's peace and joy in your heart? What's the point of receiving a promotion and making a lot of money if your big, fancy house is not a true home, but rather a boxing ring of fussing and fighting?

I have been bothered ever since I was a child by Christian testimonies that neglect the internal to focus only on outside things. "Praise God for the $100 check that came in the mail." "Praise God for sparing me from a traffic accident." While these are definitely blessings, far greater are the things God waits to do within us.

> **Our problems are not merely due to our environment; they are deeply personal. Fixing up the environment doesn't often repair the person.** ∼

God knows that our problems are not merely due to our environment; they are deeply personal. Fixing up the environment doesn't often repair the person. Some people, in fact, grow stronger in the midst of adversity; others have an easy life and still self-destruct.

SOILED ON THE INSIDE

NO ONE IN THE BIBLE wrote more honestly and eloquently about what God does inside us than David. And perhaps his most difficult piece of writing was Psalm 51.

Like all of us, David was a sinner. He gave in to pressure and temptation more than once. One spring in particular, he stayed home instead of going out with his army, and he got himself into major trouble.

And that is a warning of something I have noticed over the years: It can be dangerous not to go where God sends you, or not to do what he has called you to do. This is true for everyone, not just pastors and missionaries. I have seen choir members sing faithfully and with great effect for a while ... and then say, "I'm kind of tired; I think I'll go on leave now. Later on, I'll get involved in another ministry of the church." Carol and I have often observed that, if they don't go to the next place of service God planned for them, they eventually drift from the things of God altogether. Satan seizes that moment to reach in and distract them.

People who just hang around churches and "loiter" without getting active in the service God has called them to are in a very treacherous position. There is no difference of reward for preaching the gospel, as I have been called to do, or for serving faithfully as an usher or Christian education worker. If any of us pull back from our calling, we place ourselves at risk.

King David had too much time on his hands, and one night he couldn't sleep. Nighttime brings its own dangers. If you don't sleep well, my advice is that you had better start praising God *quickly*. Otherwise, worry, anxiety, and impure thoughts can easily creep in.

So during the night, David went out on his veranda and saw Bathsheba bathing. The woman was beautiful. He desired her—and being king, he could have anything and anyone he wanted. Everyone knows what happened next.

When Bathsheba's pregnancy became known, this "man of God" acted disgracefully. That's what sin can do to us. David called Bathsheba's husband, Uriah the Hittite, back from the battlefront in order to cover his tracks. It didn't work. So David got the man soused with liquor in a despicable attempt to sway his judgment. Even that failed. Finally, he sent Uriah back to his regiment carrying a letter to General Joab—a letter that was Uriah's own death warrant. David ordered what we New Yorkers call a "hit." He committed murder through other people's hands.

Everything was covered, David thought.

How he ever lived with himself for months and months is hard to understand. The man who had written such wonderful psalms went for most of a year with a wall between himself and God. Then God sent a prophet to confront him.

> **David ordered what we New Yorkers call a "hit." He committed murder through other people's hands.** ～

Only then did David admit his guilt. Finally we hear him come clean in Psalm 51: "Have mercy on me, O God.... Wash away all my iniquity and cleanse me from my sin" (vv. 1–2). From the depths of his soul David repents and asks pardon from the merciful God he has offended.

Then, in the middle of the psalm, David spells out three absolutely essential things that he desperately needs from God. He has learned something from his terrible fall. What he desires is impossible for him; the Lord must do it. And the work must be done *inside* him.

When you hear David's words, you will be aware of how seldom, if ever, you hear anyone pray like this in today's churches. Unfortunately, we are not asking God for things along these lines. This isn't the way we usually talk. But these three requests of David lie at the foundation of every victorious Christian life.

1. "CREATE IN ME A PURE HEART"

DAVID ASKS GOD to "create in me a pure heart" (v. 10). David is asking for more than having his sin-stained heart washed. He has already asked for cleansing (vv. 2, 7). Now he is going deeper. He wants God to start all over, to *create* a brand-new heart that is pure to the core. He admits that apart from God, he is all twisted inside. He wants to see everything in his world with pure eyes, to hear with holy ears, and to act with godly responses.

His words go far beyond our common language of "vow religion" so prominent today: "O God, I promise to do better in the future. I won't do this ever again." Some of us have turned over more new leaves than Central Park. David has no such hope in his ability to pull this off. He calls on God, instead, to create something entirely new within him. The word *create* here is the same one used in Genesis 1:1, when God created the heavens and the earth. It means a divine act of bringing something wonderful out of nothing. The work is all of God.

> **Some of us have turned over more new leaves than Central Park. David called on God, instead, to create something entirely new within him.** ～

Let me say that receiving a pure heart from God is better than getting healed of cancer. It is better than becoming rich overnight. It is better than preaching marvelous sermons or writing best-selling books. Receiving a pure heart is to be like God at the core of your being.

2. "RENEW A STEADFAST SPIRIT WITHIN ME"

THE SECOND THING David cries out for is God's steadiness in his everyday spiritual living: "Renew a steadfast spirit within me" (v. 10). We all know the feeling of being up one day and down the next ... reading the Scripture every day for a week and then hardly glancing at it the next ... going up and down like an elevator. The Hebrew word for *steadfast* means to be firm, strong, erect, immovable. What David is asking God for is a work of grace within him that will keep him from the kind of rise-and-fall, mountain-and-valley pattern that characterizes far too many of our lives. David wants to resist temptation not just one day, but every day. He knows he cannot do that himself—but with God, all things are possible.

David knows he has been cleansed and forgiven, but he feels he needs something else: a steadfast spirit. He doesn't want to be like Jell-O; he asks to be a *rock*. Isn't that our desire as well? Instead of going up and down in our walk with God, we yearn for God by his grace to do the same work for us that David sought. Do we believe God can do it?

Jesus said to Martha of Bethany, "Did I not tell you that if you believed, you would see the glory of God?" (John 11:40). We must not be content just to hope, or to lament our weak spiritual condition. Instead, we must approach the throne of grace with a bold confidence that what God promised, he will do (Hebrews 4:16). Let us ask him for this steadfast spirit that will hold us through the changing situations of life.

3. "GRANT ME A WILLING SPIRIT, TO SUSTAIN ME"

A THIRD THING that David knows he cannot manufacture on his own is "a willing spirit" (Psalm 51:12). God must grant this spirit, he admits. Beyond being steadfast, he wants to be *willing* to do whatever God asks. When God puts his finger on something in our lives and says, "That's not good for you," or "I want you to do this, or go there," we must be willing to accept his will. We can't go on fighting against God in our spirit.

David realizes that only God's power can make him willing to walk in obedience. In Philippians 2:12–13 Paul urges us to "work out your salvation with fear and trembling, for it is God who works in you *to will and to act* according to his good purpose." God is in the "willing business"—praise his name!

David has recognized that his heart can betray him. His will can consent to the appeals of the world and the flesh, so he cries out for God to give him a willing spirit. This again flies in the face of much of today's Christianity, which bites its lip and tries harder to do what only the Spirit of God can accomplish. In fact, God has to *make* us willing. Salvation is of the Lord—from beginning to end. The sooner we learn that we can stop our futile self-effort and throw ourselves on the strong arms of God, the better off we will be.

We must ask God daily to cleanse us, to hold us, to lift us up and give us a willing spirit so our hearts will "run in the path of your commands" (Psalm 119:32). Then we will actually long to do his will. We will get closer to the attitude of Jesus, who said, "My food ... is to do the will of him who sent me.... I seek not to please myself but him who sent me" (John 4:34; 5:30). It was a *joy* for Jesus to obey his Father, not a burden.

The Holy Spirit wants to impart this same spirit to us, so that Christianity is not drudgery or burdensome, but instead a life of loving the good and hating the evil.

ARE CERTAIN CHANGES IMPOSSIBLE?

HOW OFTEN HAVE you and I prayed as David did that day? Isn't it about time that we say with new faith, "God, *you* give me a pure heart. God, *you* renew a steadfast spirit within me. God, *you* grant me a willing spirit to sustain me. Don't let me fluctuate, Lord. Keep me strong!"

God is able to do this against the most vicious behavior patterns and the most embedded thoughts. Certain sins have been characterized in Christendom as almost too hard for God to change. Even ministers have said to me, "Jim, come on, tell me the truth—have you ever seen a homosexual really change?"

"What do you mean? Of course, I have!" I reply. "They are all over our church, serving in all kinds of ministries today."

> **Even ministers have said to me, "Jim, come on, tell me the truth—have you ever seen a homosexual really change?" ～**

One pastor was frank enough to tell me, "The truth is, I don't want those gays even coming to my church. Once they've been in that lifestyle, that impurity just gets engrained. I don't care who says they've been saved—I'm keeping one eye on 'em."

With that kind of unbelief and prejudice, there is little chance of witnessing the amazing grace of God in action.

One Sunday night not long ago, a very polished, intelligent man named Steve shared with our congregation what God has done in his life. Born and raised in the 'hood of southeast Washington, D.C., he nevertheless excelled in school and earned a scholarship to a Pennsylvania prep academy. While living there in his mid-teen years, he confessed to a counselor one day that he felt a vague attraction to other boys and didn't know what to think about that. The counselor answered that this was all very natural and was nothing to worry about. Steve wasn't convinced, but he said nothing more.

Steve's good grades next brought him a scholarship to the prestigious Ivy League campus of Dartmouth University in New Hampshire. His first actual homosexual experience came as a freshman at the invitation, not of an overly effeminate guy, but rather a star athlete and a candidate for the U.S. Olympic team.

"The next morning, I felt so hollow, so empty," Steve remembers. "It had been a reaching out for love, but it didn't satisfy."

Walking across campus that day to his part-time job, thinking to himself that he had certainly gotten off track, a voice suddenly said to him, *Get out of it!*

Steve did not heed the warning, however, and without any other spiritual anchor in his life, he yielded to his homosexual impulses again and again. By the time he graduated with honors from Dartmouth, he was experienced in the closet lifestyle—but still not sure if he wanted this for the rest of his life.

The lean young man with the penetrating eyes and electric smile showed talent in the field of dance, and in June 1978 he moved to New York City to accept yet another scholarship, this one at the world-renowned Alvin Ailey American Dance Center. (Eventually he landed a job with the prestigious Martha Graham Dance Company, a position he held for ten years.)

Meanwhile, a cousin challenged him to at least read the Bible, and Steve set about systematically to go through the book, starting with Genesis. It took him a year and a half to reach Revelation. During this time, he was sharing an apartment with four other dance students—all of them gay. A close camaraderie developed in the group.

"They were all very promising dancers, and they warmly took me into their circle," Steve says. "Whenever we would be talking late at night, and I'd say something about a Bible portion I had read that opposed homosexuality, they would reply, 'Oh, don't worry about that—you're reading the wrong parts. Read the Psalms, the Proverbs. God is a God of love, and anything that's loving is fine with him.'

"It made sense to me. I gradually convinced myself that my feelings for other men must be God-ordained."

LOVE OF A DIFFERENT KIND

STEVE WENT FROM ONE liaison to another, until finally a relationship solidified with a very talented artist. The two picked out an apartment to share together—one block from the Brooklyn Tabernacle. On Sundays Steve could not help noticing the crowds on the sidewalk coming in and out of our meetings, and he said to himself that he'd like to visit. In October 1980 he finally did.

"I felt the love of God the minute I came through the door," he says with a touch of amazement. "God's presence was there in a powerful way. Instinctively, I wanted to be there. When I left, I was so full of joy!"

Steve kept coming back. No one sat him down for a lecture on homosexuality. In fact, I don't think any of us knew what he was doing privately. He just kept coming to church, soaking in the Word and the presence of God—and starting to feel more and more convicted about his sin. Although he wanted to be in church, he would run out of the building immediately after the meetings, avoiding contact with other believers.

About that time, a big Gay Pride parade was scheduled in the city, and Steve's friends urged him to go. He knew he didn't want to march in the street, but he did attend the accompanying rally near the waterfront in "the Village," as we call that section of Manhattan.

"I watched the crowds of guys, arm in arm, and listened to the fervent speeches," Steve remembers, "—and I never felt so alone in all my life. Something inside my head asked, *Where will I be ten years from now? Out here 'celebrating' homosexuality in the streets? Surely not!* God was steadily chiseling away at my beliefs."

Not long after that, Steve put himself in a foolish situation one night and exposed himself to a sexually transmitted disease. That meant going to the Gay Men's Health Crisis building for a test. Once again, he felt ill at ease as he looked around the waiting room. *I don't belong here. This isn't my kind of place anymore.*

Soon Steve found himself back at our Tuesday night prayer meeting, crying out to God at a corner of the altar rail. He remembers praying, "O God, I know you love me. And I'm willing to acknowledge that this is a sin in my life. But you have to show me the way out of this. In myself, I just don't have the ability."

The struggle with his emotions continued; there was no quick exit from the gay lifestyle for Steve. He grew depressed at times and lost a lot of weight. But he was determined to believe that God would change him on the inside. In faith he held onto the promise of freedom in Christ. He made the tough decision to stop all gay activity.

Then one cloudy day on his way to work near the end of 1982, he was walking in front of the famous Bloomingdale's department store on East Fifty-Ninth Street, when, for no apparent reason, he felt a release from his bondage. "All of a sudden, I just knew that Jesus had set me free!" he says.

The relationship with his partner dissolved, and the man moved out. Steve joined a men's prayer group, where he found spiritual encouragement, and his life began to overflow with the Holy Spirit. Later he got involved with a Manhattan ministry that worked with gays and lesbians. Such Scriptures as Jeremiah 32:27 came alive to him: "I am the Lord, the God of all mankind. Is anything too hard for me?"

With his articulate speaking ability, Steve soon became a spokesman for the ministry, appearing on college campuses and Christian television shows. He was even invited to the nationally syndicated *Sally Jessie Raphael Show* for the taping of a segment called "Being Gay—Born That Way?" Predictably, he turned out to be the only Christian ex-gay on the show, and the minute he started talking about Jesus' power that had set him free, all chaos broke loose on the set. The audience howled while the other guests vented their anger toward Steve.

"On the way home that day, I was feeling sad about the whole thing. I thought of all the things I should have said that I didn't. I was pretty bummed out.

"But early the next morning, my telephone awakened me. A guy from North Carolina said, 'Were you on TV last night?'

"'Uh, yes, I was.'" (How in the world had he even found my phone number?)

"'Can Jesus really do this for someone?' the young man asked with a voice starting to crack.

"'Yes, he really can!' I replied. I went on to explain the gospel to him. Maybe my words the day before hadn't been for naught after all!"

Who Would Have Imagined?

In a few years, Steve met a beautiful young Christian woman named Desiree in our church. She also had a desire to minister to people with HIV and AIDS. In time they fell in love and began to talk about marriage.

That presented Steve with an uncomfortable dilemma. "Every partner I had had in years gone by was now dead or at least HIV-positive, I knew. The professional dancing field has been devastated by AIDS. If this thing with Desiree was to go anywhere, I knew I would have to take another test.

"The two-week wait for the results was pure agony for me. Finally the day came. I went to the clinic to hear what had been learned. The verdict was—*negative!* What an act of God's grace that I had not been infected all those years! I left the building weeping for joy."

Steve and Desiree were married June 3, 1989. Desiree knew everything there was to know about Steve—and never flinched. She left a successful sales position and returned to school to earn a master's degree in public health. Soon they started a new ministry in our church, a support group in their home for people with HIV and AIDS. Many were led to the Lord and taught that living for Christ is far more than just gritting your teeth and sitting on your hands. It is walking in faith and joy according to God's plan, which is infinitely better.

Leading the group, of course, also meant coping with loss. In one particular year, fifteen members died with AIDS.

Most recently, Steve and Desiree have moved out of the city a couple of hours away so he could accept an assistant professorship at a well-known East Coast college. Two darling little girls have been born to grace their home as more evidence of God's wonderful love. God's hand is on this couple and their children in a special way.

There is not a doubt in my mind that this wonderful man has been changed by the power of God. He told me once that while attending the National Religious Broadcasters Convention in Washington, D.C., a Christian minister came up to him on the exhibit floor and asked a few things about his work. Then he said to Steve a variation of the same question I mentioned earlier that had been posed to me: "So, you mean to tell me you've been set free from homosexuality?"

"Yes, praise the Lord!" Steve answered with a bright smile. "It's been a tremendous thing that God has done in my life."

The man looked him squarely in the face and dropped his bombshell: *"I don't believe it."* With that, he turned on his heels and walked away, leaving Steve speechless.

I am glad I wasn't there at that moment; some of the "Brooklyn" that's still in me might have come out. But a better reply to that pitiful man would have been what the apostle Paul wrote in Romans 3:3–4. "What if some did not have faith? Will their lack of faith nullify God's faithfulness? Not at all! Let God be true, and every man a liar."

> **No matter how deep and dark the secret, no matter how many times a certain sin has defeated you, God can bring change to your life.** ～

God's grace goes further and deeper than we can ever imagine. Steve's life is a reminder that God alone can give us what we really need: a pure heart, a steadfast and willing spirit. No matter how deep and dark the secret, no matter how many times a certain sin has defeated you, God can bring change to your life. But it must be his Holy Spirit working from within and not your weak attempts to "do better the next time." All God asks of you is to bring the whole, sorry mess to him so he can begin the spiritual transformation you need.

Don't attempt to be strong in yourself, for that is the very opposite of what is needed. God is always drawn to weakness. "The sacrifices of God are a broken spirit; a broken and contrite heart, O God, you will not despise" (Psalm 51:17). That verse is from the same psalm with which this chapter started, and if you will join David in his unusual prayer of faith, you will find that God's deeper work will become real in you.

TWELVE

~

Addition by Subtraction

WHEN ANY OF US goes to buy a piece of fine silver jewelry, we walk into an attractive store with aesthetic lighting and well-dressed personnel waiting to show us the various wares inside their glass cases. Everything about the surroundings is clean and sophisticated.

If we were to track that metal back to its origins, however, the opposite would be true. A silver mine is a dark, dirty, dangerous place. Men dreaming of fortunes have lost their lives in mines like Nevada's Comstock Lode during the 1859 silver rush, the Real de Monte y Pachuca in Hidalgo, Mexico (largest silver mine in the world), or the ancient sources of silver in Greece and Armenia during Bible times.

When the ore is brought to the surface, the work is far from over. The crushing, amalgamating, and smelting is still yet to be done. Silver does not melt until it reaches 960.5 degrees Celsius; only then does it start to yield up its impurities. Both King Solomon and the prophet Isaiah had all that in mind when they wrote about God's purging process, the purifying of our hearts and lives:

> Remove the dross from the silver,
>   and out comes material for the silversmith;
> remove the wicked from the king's presence,
>   and his throne will be established through
>   righteousness (Proverbs 25:4–5).

I [God] will turn my hand against you;
    I will thoroughly purge away your dross
    and remove all your impurities (Isaiah 1:25).

While all of us want our fine jewelry to be of high quality, we do not often think about the need for a similar process in our hearts. In fact, every year it is getting harder to talk about topics such as this one, because our churches have become conditioned by the world. "Feel good" and "Keep it positive" have become the operative slogans. We tend to bristle at the idea of God wanting to make major changes in our lives. We like it well enough when God says things such as "I will never leave you or forsake you . . . I will bless your coming in and your going out" and so forth. Yes, God did say all those things—but the spiritual realities are a little more complex than that.

> **"Feel good" and "Keep it positive" have become the operative slogans. We tend to bristle at the idea of God wanting to make major changes. ～**

God deals with us as a responsible parent deals with a child. Sometimes you give a compliment or a pat on the back; however, at other times you do what the apostle Paul told the young minister Timothy to do: "Correct, rebuke and encourage—with great patience and careful instruction" (2 Timothy 4:2). We like certain parts of that verse but are not so thrilled about the rest; we appreciate the "encourage" aspect and the part about "great patience," but we are not so keen about the correcting and rebuking business.

Pastors today are viewed as doing their jobs properly only when they are giving "a kind word." How many sermons and counseling sessions contain inspired correcting or rebuking? In too many places, the clergy have been reduced to hirelings—and they will only stay popular (and employed?) if they keep giving messages the people *want* to hear.

LESS IS MORE

BUT GOD'S WAY IN Scripture is far different from the ways of the American church culture. He knows the absolute necessity of removing the dross from our silver, of heating us up to an uncomfortable point where he can, as the New Living Translation puts it, "skim off your slag" (Isaiah 1:25). He is subtracting in order to add. That is strange mathematics, I admit, but it is reality in the spiritual realm. In God's math, you sometimes get more by having less.

I mentioned in my first book that when my wife and I first came to the Brooklyn Tabernacle in 1972, the church was in disarray. Fewer than twenty people came to the services. Within a month or two, I realized that some of the major problems lay within the tiny group itself! A few did whatever popped into their heads during the services. It was both unbiblical and unedifying. There were other problems with racial tension and with people insisting upon lead positions.

I was young and nervous to face this. I guess my predecessor had felt it was best to do nothing; any correction would probably drive someone away, and then the attendance (as well as the offerings) would be even smaller. But I knew in my heart that wouldn't work. I had played enough basketball to know that sometimes in order to win, you have to kick a guy off the team. The problem player may be spoiling the rhythm of the rest. He may have better-than-average talent, but in the locker room and on the floor he is a bad influence and destroys the cohesion of the team. If he won't change, he has to go. Numerous college and professional teams have experienced this. One *fewer* player sometimes means a better team.

I began to pray, "O God, either change people or have them leave." The Lord helped me to accept subtraction in order to start adding. And that is exactly what took place.

If silver is contaminated with dross, it does no good just to add more ore to the pile. The silversmith will not be able to make something beautiful out of it, no matter how large the pile or how much effort is given. Something has to be removed. As long as the impurities remain, the silver will not be shiny or smooth.

We readily accept this truth in many areas, but spiritually we resist it. Imagine someone who is eighty or a hundred pounds overweight going to the doctor and saying, "Please make me feel better. When I wake up in the morning, I'm just dragging. Give me some pills to pep me up."

The doctor would say, "All the pills in the world aren't going to restore your energy. What you need to concentrate on is losing fifty pounds, just for starters."

"What? Hey, I came here to your office to feel better! I can't change my whole lifestyle. Just give me something to help me."

The person *will* be healthier—by subtracting, not adding.

Imagine another patient, with a cancerous growth, who comes in wanting better aspirin to dull the pain. That won't work; the growth has to be cut out. If the patient protests, "Look, I didn't come in here to lose part of my body!" the doctor would reply, "Well, you *need* to lose this particular part of your body. It's cancer; it's got to go."

"You mean you care about me and say you're my friend, and you're going to cut me with a knife?"

"Exactly! If I don't, you're going to die."

TELLING THE TOUGH TRUTH

MANY OF US ARE quick to shout Hallelujah and celebrate God's blessings. Others of us have a sound intellectual grasp of Bible doctrine. That is all good—but we can easily avoid the fact that all the noise and knowledge in the world will take us nowhere if there is unremoved dross in our lives. All the talking in the world won't produce a godly life without the Lord's intimate, ongoing refining process in our hearts.

Some of us are overextended financially. Others of us have a calendar that is way too busy. The only way to get healthy is to reduce the indebtedness, to cut back the busyness. Whatever clutters our walk with God becomes the target of his purging process.

> **All the noise and knowledge in the world will take us nowhere if there is unremoved dross in our lives.** ~

So many of us think that the more we do and the more we acquire, the happier we will be. Wrong! This is why so many Christians do not see God's purposes worked out in their lives. They can quote the Bible verse about the peace of God that passes all understanding, but they have little experience of what it means.

Because God loves you, he will always be direct with you. He tells you the truth. He is absolutely ruthless in going after the things that spoil the flow of his grace and blessing into our lives. His process is to subtract in order to add. He will never make a treaty with our secret pockets of sin. "That has to go," he will insist. "You cannot go on with that in your life. I cannot make a beautiful silver vessel with that dross still present."

When Jesus began his public ministry, one of his first stops according to the Gospel of John (see chapter 2) was the cluttered temple. Did Jesus bring new paint colors and expensive furniture to add to the decor? No. He got rid of things that didn't belong there, and he kicked out the profiteering merchants. He showed himself to be a tough refiner that day, because he deeply loved the purpose of the temple as "a house of prayer for all nations," and he wanted it to be restored.

> **Because God loves you, he will always be
> direct with you. He tells you the truth. ～**

We have to face the fact that in order to be what God wants us to be, he will have to take away things in our life that don't belong. In any life or ministry devoted to him, we must stop and ask, "Are there attitudes here that grieve the Lord? Are there habits that need to be broken? What are the impurities that must go? How about that desire to be seen, that competitiveness, that seeking for glory and acclaim? What about that prejudice or judgmentalism toward others?" We must be absolutely open in inviting God to thoroughly search us and take away anything he sees fit.

One Saturday night I was seeking God in preparation for the next day's meetings, just making a fresh consecration of my life and trying to draw nearer to the Lord, when all of a sudden the names of three people came into my mind. None of them were nearby; they were scattered across the country. In all three cases, my relationship with them was not what it should have been. Nothing on the surface was wrong; I was on speaking terms with all of them. But it wasn't right before the God who is love. I didn't feel I had actually sinned against them, but still. . . .

Jim, the Lord seemed to say, *you know there's a wall between you and each of these people. Something isn't right. Call them up! You need to repair the breach.*

I quickly defended myself: "Look, I'm not the cause of these problems. I honestly feel that they are the ones with wrong attitudes, not me."

But God would not back off: *Call them and repent of any hurt you've caused, whether you meant it or not.*

Within the next week, I made the three phone calls. The humbling was good for me, and I learned new insights into God's ways of dealing in my life. What a blessing it turned out to be as I let God bring that slag to the surface and finally skim it off. Immediately afterward, I studied, prayed, and preached with a new vigor.

UNCOMFORTABLE BUT NECESSARY

LISTEN TO THE PIERCING prophecy by Malachi about Christ: "But who can endure the day of his coming? Who can stand when he appears? For he will be like a refiner's fire or a launderer's soap. He will sit as a refiner and purifier of silver; he will purify the Levites and refine them like gold and silver. Then the LORD will have men who will bring offerings in righteousness, and the offerings of Judah and Jerusalem will be acceptable to the LORD, as in days gone by, as in former years" (3:2–4).

Does your theology include Jesus sitting on a refiner's stool, watching over a cauldron of liquid metal under which the fire is getting hotter and hotter? Can you see him reaching down with a flat ladle from time to time to skim off the impurities that have bubbled to the surface? Is our faith deep enough to yield to the refiner's fire?

Will we always be comfortable in this process? Of course not! Is it pleasant? Not at all. But it is our Savior's method of getting rid of the junk in our lives. And his joy and peace will be felt immediately afterward—far deeper within us than we have ever known.

If you are a parent, you might know what it is to see too much junk food going into your child's mouth and decide to do something about it. Or maybe your child is being affected by some bad influences at school. When you take action, it doesn't exactly make you popular—but you do whatever you can to *subtract* these things from your child's life. You're not trying to rain on your child's parade; you do it because you love him.

The Bible says that "the LORD disciplines those he loves, as a father the son he delights in" (Proverbs 3:12). God's purpose for us is a lot deeper than just how we feel at the moment. He lovingly permits pressures and trials, lets the bottom fall out from time to time, so that our wrong reactions come right to the surface. We see our lack of faith, our lack of love—and that is his aim.

God intentionally places us in situations in which we are beyond our ability to cope. He permits difficulties to come with our children, and we say, "Why, God?" He is refining us. He is teaching us to trust him. He is drawing us away from our strength to his. He knows exactly how much heat to allow in our lives. He will never scorch us, but if we jump out of one cauldron because it's too hot, he has others waiting. The dross *must* be removed.

Do you know how the ancient refiner knew when he was finished, and the heat could finally be turned down? It was when he looked into the cauldron and *saw his own reflection* in the shining silver. As long as the image was muddy and rippled with flecks of slag, he knew he had to keep working. When his face finally showed clearly, the silver had been purified.

This is exactly how it is with our spiritual refining process. God's eternal plan is for us "to be conformed to the likeness of his Son" (Romans 8:29). Jesus Christ continues today as the Refiner and Purifier of his people. As he carefully works on our lives, he keeps looking into us to see his own blessed reflection.

Shall we not trust Christ and surrender to this process, rather than fighting it? Remember that it is a process of love to bring beauty and growth and enlargement in our lives. It is God's way of sanctifying us. And we must never forget that the holier the life, the more true happiness we experience within. It is the spiritual impurities that rob us of God's best.

DON'T FIGHT THE PROCESS

LET US FACE the fact that God will never let us remain the way we are today. That is the reason for this refining process in our lives. We are all "under construction." (Sometimes when I see all the major work still needed in my life, I feel like warning people to put on hard hats around me in case of falling debris.)

> **God will never let us remain the way we are today. That is the reason for this refining process in our lives.** ∼

We only move ahead by losing some things. God still adds by subtraction. Communion with him is our greatest need—but there are an awful lot of hindrances to that, aren't there? Some folks know more about *Home Improvement* than God's process of spiritual improvement for their lives. They're more up to date on sports teams and heroes than on what the apostles and prophets taught in the name of the Lord. These weights slow us down as we try to run the race of faith. We stagger at God's promises because our hearts are clogged with so many unedifying habits and unnecessary things.

When someone stubbornly fights God's purifying process, things can turn ugly. When the dross and impurities are grasped tightly like some kind of treasure, the future turns dark and foreboding. It is a kind of spiritual self-destruction.

We have had our share of spiritual shipwrecks at the Brooklyn Tabernacle. Many years ago, I lost one of my closest associates who, unknown to me, had begun to spend far too much time with a married woman who was a new Christian. His wife slowly began to sense that something was wrong, but he cleverly justified his actions on spiritual grounds and blamed her for being judgmental. She didn't share her suspicions with anyone else.

The church was much smaller then, and this associate was known and loved by all the congregation. One day in a staff meeting, I asked him to lead us in prayer. He stumbled along for a while and then broke down emotionally. Something was going on—some deep conflict of the soul. I regret to this day that I was not more discerning. I didn't confront him as a friend and brother in Christ.

Within a few months, the spiritual infection grew stronger and more ominous. Suddenly I received a phone call—while on vacation, no less—that I should quickly get back to Brooklyn. My associate had disappeared along with his lady friend, leaving behind her two children and her husband. They had taken $10,000 from the church account. They left behind a pitiful note assuring me that "God understands what we are doing."

What a tragedy! And how mightily sin can deceive.

Because this associate had been so visible, I faced the unenviable task of breaking the news as best I could to the congregation on Sunday. I broke down openly as I spoke. I can still remember the audible groans and anguished weeping throughout the church auditorium.

I have often thought how many times God must have dealt with my friend. How many times must he have been warned by the Holy Spirit? How many nights did he lie in bed fighting off the conviction of sin? We all know how persistent the Holy Spirit is when he tries to save us from the disaster of shipwreck.

I don't care how many millions around the world may have become fascinated with the story of the *Titanic* and the fateful night it sank into the cold waters of the North Atlantic. It was child's play compared with the spiritual tragedy of men and women who shun the purging of the Refiner's fire, only to find themselves in cold and dark places they never imagined.

God, I ask you to cleanse and purify our hearts and lives. Melt the dross; remove the impurities—all of it, whether in deed, word, or thought. Save us from ourselves, and establish us in righteousness by your strong right hand. We ask this humbly, depending on you, in Jesus' name. Amen.

THIRTEEN

~

The Atmosphere of Faith

THE BATTLE OF THE Christian life has always been not just to believe, but to *keep on* believing. This is how we will grow strong in faith and see the actual fulfillment of God's promises in our lives.

Throughout this book we have seen the biblical primacy of faith and its vital nature if we are to live in the will of God. The writer of Hebrews sums this up in a very famous passage:

> So do not throw away your confidence; it will be richly rewarded. You need to persevere so that when you have done the will of God, you will receive what he has promised. For in just a very little while,
>
> "He who is coming will come and will not delay.
> But my righteous one will live *by faith*.
> And if he shrinks back,
> I will not be pleased with him."

But we are not of those who shrink back and are destroyed, but of those who *believe* and are saved (10:35–39).

In other words, the writer is telling us not to be like the Israelites who believed for a while and then fell away. What doomed them from ever entering the Promised Land was not the sin of idolatry per se, or immorality, or greed—it was the horrible offense of unbelief. Though God had promised the land to the men and women delivered out of Egypt, they never put one foot in it due to their chronic lack of faith.

> **Faith is like the hand that reaches up to receive what God has freely promised. If the devil can pull your hand back down to your side, then he has succeeded.** ∿

Today we tend to soft-pedal unbelief as little more than a common weakness. We say things such as "You know, Mrs. Smith just has a hard time believing that God will help her." God takes no such easygoing approach. He calls it "shrinking back" and lets us know that he is definitely displeased. In fact, to reject his promises to us is far more destructive than the sensational sins we often talk about. The Bible calls it a "sinful, unbelieving heart that turns away from the living God" (Hebrews 3:12). Those are solemn, awesome words!

We see now why the great target of Satan is *to break down our faith*. He knows all too well that the righteous live by faith, so he aims at cutting our lifeline to God. Faith is like the hand that reaches up to receive what God has freely promised. If the devil can pull your hand back down to your side, then he has succeeded. All of God's intended supply will just stay where it is in heaven.

Remember that this faith is not merely a mental assent to certain truths in the Bible. Many people assume, "God said something, and in my mind I affirm that it is true—that's faith." They are wrong. Even the devil can give mental assent to the truth of many biblical facts, yet he remains Satan—our adversary. Real faith is produced when our hearts draw near to God himself and receive his promises deep within us. There, by its own divine power, his Word will work supernaturally.

The minute this kind of heart-faith starts to grow cold, we lose our capacity to receive from God. The chronic disease that afflicts us is not a lack of works or effort; it's a lack of real faith. Many times we are treating the symptom instead of the cause—the outward behavior and not its source.

We are running the race of faith. Those who drop out along the way are people who have stopped trusting the invisible God. None of us want to pull back or make a shipwreck of our lives as we observed in the previous chapter. We desire to receive not only his ultimate promise of salvation in heaven but also the many other promises he has made to us along the way. We want to live in the will of God.

And we don't have much time to accomplish this. As the Hebrews passage says, Jesus Christ is coming soon.

FAITH FOLLOWS PROMISES

IN RUNNING THIS RACE, we must never forget an important principle: Because of the unique place God has given to faith, *his grace flows along the channels of his promises—not his commands.* God's commands do indeed show his holy character and reveal our sinfulness, but that is all. They have no ability in themselves to empower us to obey—which puts us into a dilemma. How many believers worldwide are struggling this very hour with the realization that "I have the desire to do what is good, but I cannot carry it out" (Romans 7:18). It is not that we don't *know* what is right or that we don't *desire* to live that way. Our problem is the spiritual strength to obey, and the commands of God cannot impart that. In fact, it is not in the nature of the "Thou shalts" and "Thou shalt nots" to draw help from God. It is the ministry of his gracious promises to do that.

Saints down through the ages, while lying on their deathbeds, have not so much clung to the holy commands of God and the accompanying judgment to all offenders as they have rather cherished the promises and revelations concerning his great salvation through Christ:

> Therefore, there is now no condemnation for those who are in Christ Jesus. . . . For what the law was powerless to do in that it was weakened by the sinful nature, God did by sending his own Son in the likeness of sinful man to be a sin offering (Romans 8:1, 3).
>
> If we confess our sins, he is faithful and just and will forgive us our sins and purify us from all unrighteousness (1 John 1:9).
>
> To the man who does not work but trusts God who justifies the wicked, his faith is credited as righteousness (Romans 4:5).

These are the blessed promises of God that, when trusted, release his supernatural grace in and through us.

Listen to a man who often failed while depending upon his own strength, though he knew so well the commands of Christ. The apostle Peter tells us the blessed secret that God "has given us his very great and precious *promises*, so that through *them* [we] may participate in the divine nature and escape the corruption in the world caused by evil desires" (2 Peter 1:4). It is these promises that draw the heart to God in faith. This, in fact, is the great command of the New Covenant—to believe!

Without feeding on the promises of the Word, no faith life will be strong. We will not be able to continue on and persevere without living in the Word. There has never been a great man or woman of faith who was not a man or woman of the Book. My shelves are lined with such biographies as Luther, Wesley, Finney, Spurgeon, Moody—they read the Word, lived in it, meditated on it, and through its divine power working in their hearts, grew strong in faith.

> **There has never been a great man or woman of faith who was not a man or woman of the Book.** ～

Of course, you will not succeed with only the words on the page. The Israelites who left Egypt came up short with regard to God's promise of possessing that new land for this reason: "The message they heard was of no value to them, because those who heard did not combine it with faith" (Hebrews 4:2). They heard clearly what God promised, but their hearts did not receive it in faith.

Today it is possible to make a living as an esteemed theologian and yet have no more living faith than a slug. Christians can sit in pews listening to the Word preached every Sunday—and even have a devotional life of sorts throughout the week—without rising above the cynicism, depression, and unbelief that are so prevalent in our culture. We can know the Word in some sense, but the Word must find within our hearts an atmosphere in which its divine power can be released.

That kind of dynamic faith fairly oozes from the words of the great Israelite leader Joshua near the end of his life. He was one of only two men who left Egypt as adults and actually *made* it all the way into the Promised Land. Listen to Joshua's parting instructions, which reveal the atmosphere of faith—the environment in which it blossoms and grows.

LOOK BACK WITH THANKSGIVING

JOSHUA BEGINS HIS FAREWELL address with this ringing statement: "You yourselves have seen everything the LORD your God has done to all these nations for your sake; it was the LORD your God who fought for you" (Joshua 23:3). In other words, look back, fellow Israelites, and think about all he has done.

How about *us* recalling right now all that God has done for *us* just in the past twelve months? How many hundreds of mornings did you wake up with strength in your limbs to get up and function? You didn't manufacture the strength yourself; it was a gift from God. When did you last thank God for your mental alertness, for a functional memory, or for the skills to be able to hold a job? "Every good and perfect gift is from above, coming down from the Father" (James 1:17). We forget that truth too often. How can we have faith for the future if we don't often look back and thank God for all he's given us in the past?

We have become numb to his many benefits. More than half the persons on this globe have never had the experience of making a telephone call! What we take for granted as an everyday convenience is unknown to much of the planet. A lack of gratitude is, in fact, one of our besetting sins. In most of our churches, there is no outpouring of vibrant thanksgiving and praise each Sunday because we are too occupied with our problems. We concentrate on what we don't have rather than "enter[ing] his gates with thanksgiving and his courts with praise" (Psalm 100:4).

One day in the lobby of our church, a woman named Donna said to me with great excitement, "Pastor Cymbala, I got my first studio apartment—a place of my own! Praise the Lord!" I began to rejoice with her over the simple blessing that she now actually had a one-room place to live. You might find that a little strange ... but then you don't know where Donna was coming from. Several weeks before, the police had gathered outside our church because a "jumper" seemed determined to end her life from a ledge on the building next to ours.

I moved outside with others of our staff and saw Donna high in the air. She had just left the office of her therapist in that building, who obviously had not provided the answer she needed. She was both anguished and frightened at the same time.

I felt God prompt me to enter the building and run up the stairs to where the officers were trying to talk Donna off the ledge. The panicked therapist stood by helplessly. I asked for permission to speak to her, but the cops warned me not to grab for her if I got close, because she might pull me down with her to the pavement.

In about twenty minutes, God helped me to bring her off the ledge into my arms. A staff member went with her in the ambulance for the required examination at a local hospital. We found out later that she had been staying either on a friend's couch or with a man who was abusive to her. Her life had been very sad, but she soon received Christ as her Savior. We helped her find some temporary lodging. When Donna got to the point of being able to rent her own room, believe me, it was a great day to give God a sacrifice of thanksgiving!

Don't you have at least as much to thank God for as Donna does? Then give him praise! Let him know from the depths of your heart how much you appreciate his goodness. Open up your heart and your mouth. Whether it is part of your religious tradition or not, the Bible tells you to express the gratitude of your heart toward the Lord. Get past your self-consciousness and formality to praise the Lord. Refuse to be embarrassed or hindered by anyone.

How pitiful that millions of churchgoers cheer wildly and unashamedly for their favorite sports teams—but are silent as a corpse when it comes to praising God! Read the Bible about the decibel level in heaven. How comfortable will you feel amid the sounds of saints and angels "numbering thousands upon thousands, and ten thousand times ten thousand ... in a *loud* voice they sang, 'Worthy is the Lamb ...!'" (Revelation 5:11–12)? Do you have the kind of worshipful, thankful heart that will want to join what John heard as "a great multitude, like the roar of rushing waters and like loud peals of thunder, shouting: 'Hallelujah! For our Lord God Almighty reigns'" (19:6)? May God help us to praise him more!

> **How pitiful that millions of churchgoers cheer wildly and unashamedly for their favorite sports teams—but are silent as a corpse when it comes to praising God!** ～

Think of the many times we have found ourselves in some kind of a bind and have prayed with desperation, "O God, please—if you'll just help this time, I'll serve you and thank you and honor you forever." If that is your history, then don't forget what God has done. Rather, "through Jesus, therefore, let us continually offer to God a sacrifice of praise— the fruit of lips that confess his name" (Hebrews 13:15).

LOOK AHEAD WITH ANTICIPATION

NEXT JOSHUA TURNS HIS attention to the future. You might think that he would be satisfied, at the end of his years, with his many achievements. The first twenty-two chapters of his book tell how he has led the Israelites in conquering vast sections of Canaan. City after city has already fallen to his troops.

But Joshua is not satisfied. He boldly proclaims, "The LORD your God himself will drive [the remaining Canaanite nations] out of your way. He will push them out before you, and you will take possession of their land, as the LORD your God promised you" (Joshua 23:5). Joshua is still, at this late age, invoking the promises of God and boldly declaring that "the LORD your God *himself* " will do the conquering.

Every one of us, if we are honest, can point to things in our lives today that are not yet the way God wants them to be. There is a good deal of "land" still to be conquered. God wants to make us more like the Savior. He wants to root out things that hinder and mar our Christlikeness. He wants to use us to bless and encourage other people in ways we have never experienced or even dreamed. He wants to destroy the complexes and fears that paralyze us. He wants to revive and bless our local church congregations.

And he *will* do these things himself as we live in this blessed atmosphere of faith!

Among the many definitions of faith, perhaps none is more succinct or important than Hebrews 11:1. "Now faith is being sure of what we hope for and certain of what we do not see."

Notice that faith operates in respect to two special objects:

- Future things ("what we hope for")
- Invisible things ("what we do not see")

Faith is not about the present. It is not about things you could capture right now with a camera. Rather, it is about things in the future promised by God—and faith is certain of them. Faith produces a conviction that those things are going to happen, even though the scientific method and our senses cannot validate that certainty at the moment.

....

Faith is not about the present. It is not about things you could capture right now with a camera. Rather, it is about things in the future promised by God. ～

....

Faith is the ability of the human spirit to open up and receive impressions from God that are born from his Word and made alive by the Holy Spirit. This brings about a supernatural conviction of certain facts apart from the senses. Andrew Murray put it this way more than a hundred years ago, "Just as we have our senses, through which we hold communication with the physical universe, so faith is the spiritual sense or organ through which the soul comes into contact with and is affected by the spiritual world."[1] In other words, just as our sense of sight or hearing lies dormant until acted upon by light or sound, so our ability to have faith lies dormant until we open ourselves to receive impressions from the eternal, invisible God.

Then we simply *know* that something is going to happen, for God's Word has been received and has activated this spiritual sense called faith. We now bank our life on it. If somebody says, "Prove it," we cannot—but we still know it is coming.

This is what Moses experienced thousands of years ago. "By faith he left Egypt, not fearing the king's anger; he persevered *because he saw him who is invisible*" (Hebrews 11:27).

How do you see the invisible? Not with the eyes in your head, but with the more powerful eyes of faith.

The senses—touch, taste, smell, sight, hearing—have to do with present and visible things. They can't pick up anything about the future. They have nothing to do with spiritual realities. But faith has to do primarily with these future and invisible things that God has promised us in his Word. Faith makes them more real to us than the headlines of today's newspaper. This other kind of "seeing" is what faith is all about, as the apostle Paul says in 2 Corinthians 4:18: "So we fix our eyes not on what is seen, but on what is unseen. For what is seen is temporary, but what is unseen is eternal."

Faith can be likened to a transistor radio. When you turn the radio on, music pours out. Are there any trumpets or guitars inside that little box? Of course not. Yet the room has sound waves all through it. The human senses can't detect them at all. But the radio can pick them up. The music is not actually in the radio at all. The music is coming *through* the radio from a greater unseen source.

So it is with faith. Faith does not originate within us. It comes from God as we receive his living Word into our hearts. Then a supernatural kind of "music" comes alive in us as the product of this faith. A person filled with faith has an entirely different view of things from the person living merely by the physical senses.

Back in the most difficult days of the Brooklyn Tabernacle, when Carol and I had just come to the little church and were struggling to stay afloat with maybe forty people attending on Sunday mornings, our daughter Chrissy was about two years old. One morning at the breakfast table, we noticed a lump under her eyelid. The next day it seemed bigger. We didn't talk about it, even though the lump grew steadily larger.

"What do you think it is?" Carol finally asked one day with worry in her voice.

"I don't know."

"We'd better take her to a doctor," she said. The trouble was, we had no health insurance.

That night I spent time praying about the problem, and the longer I prayed, the more ominous it seemed. Did my little girl have some kind of tumor that would steal her eyesight? I said the right words to God, but I knew there was no faith in my heart. There was only apprehension.

We scraped up the money, and I took her to a doctor. He confirmed, "Yes, this is a growth—[he gave the technical name]—that shouldn't be there. It's not life-threatening, but we will need to cut it out."

The thought of my little firstborn daughter having a knife only millimeters from her eye immediately frightened me. Additionally, I was concerned how we would ever pay for the surgery.

That night, after Chrissy went to sleep, I returned to her room. I picked her up and held her in my arms. I prayed quietly, "O God, heal my daughter."

> **As I stood there in the semidarkness, holding my child and staring at the lump under her eye, I was filled with doubt and fear. I needed true, living faith. ～**

Once again, although I was saying prayer-words, all I could see was a lump that now seemed as large as a boulder. I knew what God had said in the Bible about healing—I had preached from those texts. A dramatic healing had even played a role long ago in my grandmother coming to Christ.

But as I stood there in the semidarkness, holding my child and staring at the lump under her eye, I was filled with doubt and fear. I needed true, living faith, not theoretical faith.

The following Sunday, after the sermon, we were singing and worshiping together at the end of the service. I led the people in praising God for his goodness, while Carol played the organ. Suddenly my heart was flooded with a kind of divine light that brought a new sense of God powerfully to my soul.

I was overcome with God's awesome greatness, which makes everything on earth seem miniscule. Then suddenly— as God is my witness, I am not embellishing the story—I *saw* my daughter being prayed for at the front of the church. *And I saw her being healed!* It was not emotional or spooky; it was a real and definite picture before the eyes of my heart. God had birthed something within me.

My heart was pounding with joy as I reached for the microphone. "Who is holding my daughter?" I asked. (Our church was far too small back then to have an organized nursery.)

A teenage girl's hand went up in the back.

"Bring her up here quickly," I said. We gathered around her and anointed her with oil, praying together for God to heal her.

Within forty-eight hours, the lump was entirely gone, with no surgery, no doctor, no medical intervention of any kind. The God who longs to do great things for his people was encouraging us once again to believe.

Now what would happen in your church or mine if people came to each meeting with greater faith—a spirit of anticipation, a belief that God was about to do something wonderful? This was the very expectancy that greeted Jesus in many places. People fought just to touch him, for they *knew* something wonderful would happen. What if *we* yielded our hearts to both his Word and his Spirit instead of just mechanically repeating the same old order of service we have been following for the past twenty years? Something tells me things would never be the same.

Unfortunately, I have learned firsthand that many Christians who pound the Bible the hardest and most strongly defend the verbal inspiration of Scripture are the most unbelieving and cynical about God ever doing a new thing in his church. They seem so intent on preserving tradition that any spontaneity is spurned as "emotionalism." My question is: If Jesus is the same today as he was in the Bible we defend, why shouldn't we believe him to do great things among us and through us, so we can touch people's lives in powerful ways as did the first-century apostles? Peter was no perfect saint, as evidenced by his denial of Christ; many churches today would hardly allow such a failure to stand in their pulpits. But God chose him on the Day of Pentecost and used him mightily—and God can do the same with us if we look to him with childlike faith in our hearts.

> **Many Christians who pound the Bible the hardest are the most unbelieving and cynical about God ever doing a new thing in his church. ～**

More than twenty-five years ago, David Wilkerson preached a great sermon called "God Only Uses Failures." Of course, it's true—what else does God have to work with? But if we dare to believe him, we can be valuable instruments in his hand.

Look Inward — But Carefully

Next, Joshua calls the people to take stock of their obedience: "Be very strong; be careful to obey all that is written in the Book of the Law of Moses, without turning aside to the right or to the left. Do not associate with these nations that remain among you; do not invoke the names of their gods or swear by them. You must not serve them or bow down to them. But you are to hold fast to the LORD your God, as you have until now" (Joshua 23:6–8).

This separation from ungodly things was for the purpose of the Hebrews' maintaining their strength for battle. Alliance with sinful things—even just questionable practices—saps our strength and leaves us weak before the enemy. If there are some wrong conversations going on, an inappropriate relationship, or some fascination with a questionable topic or thing, we slowly but surely undercut our spiritual vitality. The enemy has subtly stolen our "shield of faith" needed to protect us in "the day of evil" (Ephesians 6:13, 16).

Joshua knew this all too well from what had happened back at Ai (see Joshua 7). After the stirring victory at Jericho, the disobedience of one soldier named Achan clogged up the carburetor of the whole Israelite war engine. The army suffered an unexpected and humiliating defeat—not because God had lost his power, but because something had separated the people from his holy companionship. Joshua had to stop everything and root out the sin before the military campaign took another step.

The apostle John wrote, "Do not love the world or anything in the world. If anyone loves the world, the love of the Father is not in him. For everything in the world—the cravings of sinful man, the lust of his eyes and the boasting of what he has and does—comes not from the Father but from the world" (1 John 2:15–16). Love for the world and preoccupation with its sick value system and enticements will wreck anyone's faith life.

Introspection, of course, is a two-edged sword. If we give long periods of time just to looking inward, we can easily get morose and spiritually depressed. There are special times for focusing on these things—for example, at the receiving of Communion (see 1 Corinthians 11:28–32) and other moments of divine searching within us. But if this process consumes us exclusively, Satan can easily gain the upper hand as our accuser, keeping us preoccupied with *our* failures rather than with Christ's pardon and power.

It is interesting to me that "solemn assemblies"—occasions when Old Testament leaders set aside whole days for confession and repentance and weeping—are not found in the New Testament. Yes, the apostles believed in getting right with God, in dealing with sin—but they did not grovel in it for long periods of time. Instead, it seems that they called people to cleanse their hearts before God and then moved on to faith and the fullness of the Holy Spirit. After all, Jesus left a Great Commission of work for the church to do. How would that be accomplished if his followers were continually looking inward at their own faults and shortcomings?

LOOK AWAY TO JESUS

JOSHUA'S FINAL INSTRUCTION is stated very simply: "Be very careful to love the LORD your God" (Joshua 23:11). Our gaze must always be upon him, because he is the one who will perform everything. Only when we are "looking unto Jesus, the author and finisher of our faith" (Hebrews 12:2 KJV) are we truly walking in faith.

Satan wants us to focus on the problem, not the Provider. He constantly points to what *seems* to be rather than to what God has promised to do. If we stop spending time with the Lord in prayer, the concerns of the physical world snatch our attention and dominate us, while the spiritual senses deaden and the promises fade.

> **The number one reason that Christians today don't pray more is because we do not grasp the connection between prayer and the promises of God.** ~

I am absolutely convinced that the number one reason that Christians today don't pray more is because we do not grasp the connection between prayer and the promises of God. We are trying as individuals and churches to pray "because we're supposed to" without a living faith in the promises of God concerning prayer. No prayer life of any significance can be maintained by this "ought-to" approach. There must be faith in God at the bottom.

Time and again I get phone calls and letters from hungry believers throughout the nation saying, "Pastor Cymbala, I am so frustrated—I've been to sixteen churches now in my area, and I can't find one that has a prayer meeting!" It is obvious that while pastors and leaders mentally accept the Bible's teaching on prayer, they don't really *see* its potential power through God. Otherwise, they would be leading their congregations to do it rather than just preaching sermons about it.

When real faith in God arises, a certainty comes that when we call, he will answer . . . that when we ask, we will receive . . . that when we knock, the door will be opened . . .

and soon we find ourselves spending a lot of time in his presence. We seek him for wayward children to be saved, for a greater sense of the Holy Spirit in our church services, for spiritual gifts and power to be released, for the finances we need to do his work.

But I am speaking about more than just presenting a laundry list of requests to God. Faith is especially nurtured when we just wait in God's presence, taking the time to love him and listen for his voice. Strength to keep believing often flows into us as we simply worship the Lord. The promises of Scripture become wonderfully alive as the Spirit applies them to our hearts.

> **Faith is especially nurtured when we just wait in God's presence, taking the time to love him and listen for his voice.** ～

When people come to my office overloaded with problems, not knowing where to turn, I sometimes say, "Here is what I want you to do: Go sit with the Prayer Band upstairs in their special room this Friday night from midnight to two in the morning."

They often react with shock on their faces. "Oh, Pastor Cymbala—I'm so discouraged I can't believe that the sun will come up tomorrow. I could never pray for two hours!"

"I didn't ask you to pray," I reply. "I just asked you to go sit there. The Prayer Band will pray for you. And God will operate on your heart as you just wait in his presence."

How many times have I heard back from these people that while they were sitting in that atmosphere, God brought alive his Word and his promises and lifted their spirits to believe. Thanksgiving began to flow. They began to remember the good things God had done in their past. Faith began to spring anew as they waited on the One who can so easily turn everything around in life.

GOD IS WAITING FOR YOU

WHAT DIFFICULTY ARE YOU now facing in your life that you have not been able to overcome? I wonder what God is waiting to accomplish in your life, your home, your work, your service for him. Why don't you and I face our need in Jesus' name and reach out in fresh faith to the Lord?

Let us not be hesitant or unsure about trusting him after reading all these wonderful stories and encouragements. Let us, rather, "draw near to God with a sincere heart *in full assurance of faith*, having our hearts sprinkled to cleanse us from a guilty conscience and having our bodies washed with pure water. Let us hold unswervingly to the hope we profess, for *he who promised is faithful*" (Hebrews 10:22–23). In the end, that is what really matters—not our efforts or pledges, but the wonderful truth that God is a faithful God.

So now, what will it be for all of us? Will we simply be stirred for a moment, or will we lay hold of God and his promises in a new, life-changing way? After all, it is not what happens externally to people that makes for tragedy in their lives; it is the missed opportunities to see God help them, due to their unbelief. That is the real tragedy.

God will be no different tomorrow than he is today. His love for us is the same. His power to meet our needs is unchanged. Right now his hand reaches out as he says, "Why spend money on what is not bread, and your labor on what does not satisfy?" (Isaiah 55:2). Let us stop the futile search for answers outside of God. Instead, let us arise with hope in our hearts, remembering that this powerful "word of faith" is not far away and difficult, but rather "is near you; it is in your mouth and in your heart" (Romans 10:8). This is the faith that not only saves us from sin but can also keep us victorious over every obstacle that life presents to us. "As the Scripture says, 'Anyone who trusts in him will never be put to shame'" (Romans 10:11).

Joshua must have had God's faithfulness in mind when he finished his speech that day with this great crescendo: "Now I am about to go the way of all the earth. You know with all your heart and soul that not one of all the good promises the LORD your God gave you has failed. Every promise has been fulfilled; not one has failed" (Joshua 23:14). We, too, can finish our race in life with the same powerful declaration, if we will only keep believing in the God whose promises are forever true.

EPILOGUE

~

33 Treasures

MORE VALUABLE THAN anything I could write or preach on the subject of faith are the direct declarations and promises of God's Word. Here are gems from the Bible that have inspired me over the years to believe. They have also formed the foundation for many a sermon.

As you read them, let them penetrate your mind and your spirit. Open your Bible and read the full passages in which they occur. Review them often as you seek to strengthen your own walk of faith.

~

SO THEN FAITH COMES by hearing, and hearing by the word of God.

ROMANS 10:17 NKJV

~

THE ONLY THING that counts is faith expressing itself through love.

GALATIANS 5:6

~

EVERYONE BORN OF GOD overcomes the world. This is the victory that has overcome the world, even our faith.

1 JOHN 5:4

～

THEY ASKED HIM, "What must we do to do the works God requires?"

Jesus answered, "The work of God is this: to believe in the one he has sent."

JOHN 6:28–29

～

IT IS BETTER TO take refuge in the LORD than to trust in man.

PSALM 118:8

～

FAITH IS BEING SURE of what we hope for and certain of what we do not see. This is what the ancients were commended for.

HEBREWS 11:1–2

～

WITHOUT FAITH IT IS impossible to please God, because anyone who comes to him must believe that he exists and that he rewards those who earnestly seek him.

HEBREWS 11:6

～

THE APOSTLES SAID to the Lord, "Increase our faith!"

LUKE 17:5

～

WE DO NOT WANT you to become lazy, but to imitate those who through faith and patience inherit what has been promised.

HEBREWS 6:12

∿

IF ANY OF YOU lacks wisdom, he should ask God, who gives generously to all without finding fault, and it will be given to him. But when he asks, he must believe and not doubt, because he who doubts is like a wave of the sea, blown and tossed by the wind.

JAMES 1:5–6

∿

TRUST IN THE LORD and do good;
    dwell in the land and enjoy safe pasture. . . .
Commit your way to the LORD ;
    trust in him and he will do this. . . .
Be still before the LORD and wait patiently for him;
    do not fret when men succeed in their ways,
    when they carry out their wicked schemes.

PSALM 37:3, 5, 7

∿

CAST YOUR CARES on the LORD
    and he will sustain you;
    he will never let the righteous fall.

PSALM 55:22

∿

TRUST IN HIM at all times, O people;
    pour out your hearts to him,
    for God is our refuge. *Selah*

PSALM 62:8

∿

BUT NOW, THIS IS what the LORD says—
    he who created you, O Jacob,
    he who formed you, O Israel:

"Fear not, for I have redeemed you;
    I have summoned you by name; you are mine.
When you pass through the waters,
    I will be with you;
and when you pass through the rivers,
    they will not sweep over you.
When you walk through the fire,
    you will not be burned;
    the flames will not set you ablaze."

ISAIAH 43:1–2

∾

I AM THE LORD, your God,
    who takes hold of your right hand
and says to you, Do not fear;
    I will help you.

ISAIAH 41:13

∾

TRUST IN THE LORD with all your heart
    and lean not on your own understanding.

PROVERBS 3:5

∾

WHO AMONG YOU fears the LORD
    and obeys the word of his servant?
Let him who walks in the dark,
    who has no light,
trust in the name of the LORD
    and rely on his God.

ISAIAH 50:10

∼

MY EYES ARE EVER on the LORD,
   for only he will release my feet from the snare.

PSALM 25:15

∼

TO ALL WHO received him, to those who believed in his
   name, he gave the right to become children of God.

JOHN 1:12

∼

"WHOEVER BELIEVES IN ME, as the Scripture has said,
   streams of living water will flow from within him."

JOHN 7:38

∼

"HE MADE NO DISTINCTION between us and them, for he
   purified their hearts by faith."

ACTS 15:9

∼

WHAT THEN SHALL we say that Abraham, our forefather, discovered in this matter? If, in fact, Abraham was justified by
works, he had something to boast about—but not before
God. What does the Scripture say? "Abraham believed God,
and it was credited to him as righteousness."

Now when a man works, his wages are not credited to
him as a gift, but as an obligation. However, to the man who
does not work but trusts God who justifies the wicked, his
faith is credited as righteousness.

ROMANS 4:1–5

～

AGAINST ALL HOPE, Abraham in hope believed and so became the father of many nations, just as it had been said to him, "So shall your offspring be."

ROMANS 4:18

～

CHRIST IS THE END of the law so that there may be righteousness for everyone who believes.

ROMANS 10:4

～

THEY WERE BROKEN OFF because of unbelief, and you stand by faith. Do not be arrogant, but be afraid.

ROMANS 11:20

～

... SO THAT YOUR faith might not rest on men's wisdom, but on God's power.

1 CORINTHIANS 2:5

～

IN SCRIPTURE IT SAYS:
　　"See, I lay a stone in Zion,
　　　　a chosen and precious cornerstone,
　　and the one who trusts in him
　　　　will never be put to shame."

1 PETER 2:6

～

NOT THAT WE LORD it over your faith, but we work with you for your joy, because it is by faith you stand firm.

2 CORINTHIANS 1:24

～

IN ADDITION TO ALL THIS, take up the shield of faith, with which you can extinguish all the flaming arrows of the evil one.

EPHESIANS 6:16

～

LET US DRAW NEAR to God with a sincere heart in full assurance of faith, having our hearts sprinkled to cleanse us from a guilty conscience and having our bodies washed with pure water.

HEBREWS 10:22

～

"MY RIGHTEOUS ONE will live by faith.
And if he shrinks back,
    I will not be pleased with him."

But we are not of those who shrink back and are destroyed, but of those who believe and are saved.

HEBREWS 10:38–39

～

WHEN HE HAD gone indoors, the blind men came to him, and he asked them, "Do you believe that I am able to do this?"

"Yes, Lord," they replied.

MATTHEW 9:28

～

IMMEDIATELY THE BOY'S FATHER exclaimed, "I do believe; help me overcome my unbelief!"

MARK 9:24

Notes

Chapter Five—Can I Trust God to Lead Me?

1. *The Works of John Wesley*—CD (Franklin, Tenn.: Providence House, 1995); see also "The Character of a Methodist," *The Works of John Wesley*, 3d ed., vol. 8, p. 339 (London: Wesleyan Methodist Book Room, 1872; reprinted Grand Rapids: Baker, 1996).

2. Sermon entitled "The Eternal Name," preached on the evening of May 27, 1855, at Exeter Hall, London.

Chapter Seven—Faith Runs on a Different Clock

1. "Keep Believing" by Tim Pedigo (Nashville: Meadowgreen Music, copyright © 1985).

Chapter Eight—Overcoming Discouragement

1. Cited in *Words Old and New*, compiled by Horatius Bonar (reprint Edinburgh: Banner of Truth Trust, 1994), pp. 16–17.

Chapter Thirteen—The Atmosphere of Faith

1. Andrew Murray, *The Holiest of All* (1894; reprint Grand Rapids: Revell, 1993), pp. 441–42.

～ *Fresh Wind, Fresh Fire* ～

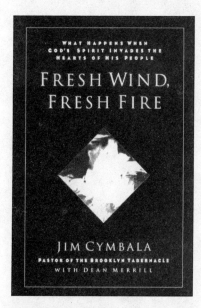

In 1972, The Brooklyn Tabernacle's spark was almost out. Then the Holy Spirit lit a fire that couldn't be quenched.

Pastor Jim Cymbala shares the lessons he learned when the Spirit ignited his heart and began to move through his people. This unforgettable story will set a fire burning in your own heart to experience God's mercy, power, and love as though for the first time.

"This is an important book for all those whose Christianity has become still and sterile. Fresh Wind, Fresh Fire signals that God is at work in our day and that he wishes to be at work in our lives."
—Dr. Joseph M. Stowell

"This book will drive you to your knees. Be prepared to be provoked but also greatly challenged. You can be sure that reading this book will change you forever." —David Wilkerson

Hardcover 0-310-21188-3
Audio Pages 0-310-21199-9

ZondervanPublishingHouse
Grand Rapids, Michigan

A Division of HarperCollinsPublishers

We want to hear from you. Please send your comments about this book to us in care of the address below. Thank you.

ZondervanPublishingHouse
Grand Rapids, Michigan 49530
http://www.zondervan.com